THE OTHER JESUS

THE OTHER
JESUS

———◆———

A Narrative Based on
Apocryphal Stories Not Included
in the Bible

ARRANGED, EDITED, AND WITH COMMENTS BY
ROBERT O. BALLOU

Doubleday & Company, Inc.
Garden City, New York
1972

The author is grateful to the following for the use of copyrighted material:
The Clarendon Press, Oxford, England, for material from *The Apocryphal New Testament* by M. R. James, 1924.

Doubleday & Company, Inc., for material from *The Secret Sayings of Jesus* by Robert M. Grant and David Noel Freedman, copyright © 1960 by Robert M. Grant and David Noel Freedman. Reprinted by permission of Doubleday & Company, Inc.

Vincent Stuart & John M. Watkins Ltd., London, for material from *Fragments of a Faith Forgotten* by G. R. S. Mead, 1931.

The Westminster Press for material from *New Testament Apocrypha*, Volume One, edited by Edgar Hennecke and Wilhelm Schneemelcher. English translation edited by R. McL. Wilson. Published in the U.S.A. by The Westminster Press, 1963. Copyright © 1959, J. C. B. Mohr (Paul Siebeck), Tübingen. English translation © 1963, Lutterworth Press, London. Used by permission.

CONTENTS

I believe in God, the Father Almighty,
creator of heaven and earth, and in
Jesus Christ, his only Son, our Lord;
who was conceived by the Holy Ghost,
born of the Virgin Mary, suffered under
Pontius Pilate, was crucified, died,
and was buried. He descended into Hell;
the third day he arose again from the dead;
He ascended into heaven, and sits at the
right hand of God, the Father Almighty;
thence he shall come to judge
the living and the dead.
I believe in the Holy Ghost,
the Holy Catholic Church,
the communion of saints,
the forgiveness of sins,
the resurrection of the body,
and life everlasting. Amen.

The Apostles' Creed.

INTRODUCTION

THAT PART OF THE STORY of, and comments on, Jesus of Nazareth that occurs in the familiar Gospels, Acts, and Epistles of the New Testament of the Judeo-Christian Bible constitutes a smaller body of literature than that in other sources. Much, though not all, of the extracanonical literature is in what is known as "The New Testament Apocrypha," and extracts from a number of the many books that constitute this collection form the major part of the present volume. Other sources, however, have also been used, and identified.

The terms "apocrypha" and "apocryphal" have meant to many something false or without foundation in fact. In the earlier centuries of their use, however, they had a much more dignified and inviting meaning, being applied to material that was held to be too sacred to be available to everyone, and thus, something secret. Several of the Old Testament books that have been included under the general term "apocryphal," however, contain no secret lore whatever.

As to the meaning "false," *The Oxford Dictionary of the Christian Church,* under the heading "Apocryphal New Testament," says, "The epithet 'apocryphal' here does not of itself imply inaccuracy, unauthenticity or unorthodoxy."

What then does the word mean? Actually only that the books and fragments to which it has been applied, among the many that were written during the early centuries of the Christian era, are not included in the conventional Bible, known as the

Canon, of the Christian Church. The books of the Old Testament Apocrypha (The Three Holy Children, The Wisdom of Solomon, Bel and the Dragon, First and Second Maccabees, Susanna and the Elders, Baruch, Judith, Tobit, First and Second Esdras, et al.) are fairly well known and are included in some Bibles between the Old and New Testaments. The New Testament Apocrypha has never been a part of the Canon (though a number of its books were given credence before the Canon was crystallized), and is very little known to the general reader. It consists of a number of gospels, acts, epistles, and apocalypses, most of which were written between the first and fourth centuries A.D. Their purpose, according to M. R. James,[1] was to "reinforce the existing stock of Christian beliefs: either revealing new doctrines—usually differing from those which held the field; or by interpreting old ones—again, usually in a fresh sense; or by extolling some special virtue, as chastity or temperance; or by enforcing belief in certain doctrines or events, e.g., the Virgin birth, the Resurrection of Christ, the second coming, the future state—by the production of evidence which, if true, should be irrefragable." In short, they were, to put the matter bluntly, propaganda for the infant Christian Church.

Actually, however, this could also be said for the books of the canonical New Testament. The difference is one of degree rather than kind. The literary quality and credibility of the canonical books are, in general, higher than those of the Apocrypha, but this, again, is a matter of degree rather than kind, and perhaps the difference in degree of credibility is somewhat dependent upon the difference in literary quality.

Yet there is much in the apocryphal books associated with the New Testament that is beautiful, wise, and reverent.

As to authority, a comparison of the dates of the books of the canonical New Testament with those of the New Testament apocryphal books would accord a larger degree of authenticity, perhaps, to the canonical books, if only because, in general, they are earlier. Yet several of the apocryphal books are little, if any, later than the latest date assigned to the writing of the latest of the canonical gospels—The Gospel according to John.

The value of all biblical literature as conventional history is strongly suspect, for it is inevitably colored with the mysticism and emotionalism that is almost invariably inseparable from religious belief. Yet it has a special value of its own in its revelation of the religious intensities of the times during which it was written and the thinking of the peoples whose faith it records. The books of the New Testament Apocrypha in no way negate this truth. Their number, far exceeding those of the canonical New Testament and the Judeo-Christian Old Testament together—perhaps as many as two hundred and fifty, according to scholarly estimates, some of which are known only through references to them by early Christian writers, and many others of which are extant only as fragments—attest the tremendous impact the angry young man of Nazareth, aflame with wrath against hypocrisy, cruelty, and hatred that supplanted love, must have had on the world at the time in which he lived, an impact that was continued by the Pauline missionaries after his death, and the passionate devotion of the young Christian church to the mystique of Jesus, from whose life as a god-man (in the view of the Christians), his teaching, and his death on the cross, had been born a new religion that demanded complete mental, emotional, and spiritual commitment from its adherents.

The spread of the apocryphal literature throughout the world of the first few centuries of the Christian era is also impressive. Fragments of texts have been recovered in Hebrew, Greek, Latin, Syriac, Coptic, Arabic, Ethiopic, and in several medieval vernaculars. There were books of gospels, of acts, of epistles, and of apocalypses in the infant world of Christianity, the doctrines of which were a mixed heritage.

In order to understand the situation which gave rise to these many books that have not become a part of our Bible, yet are concerned with those same important matters that fill our New

Testament, it is necessary to know the state of religion in general during the period in which the apocryphal books were written.

It would be a mistake to think of Christianity during the first three centuries of its existence as a single, homogeneous religion. Indeed it is not that today, though the differences between the denominations or even between the two mainstreams of Roman Catholicism and Protestantism are much less than those that produced innumerable communities and innumerable expressions of faith as the appealing story of Jesus of Nazareth spread throughout the Mediterranean region. In the swelling current that was to become known as Christianity were merged streams from Israel, Egypt, Greece, and from various aspects of the older faiths of these cultures. These same streams—especially those from Greece and Egypt, had, before the crucifixion of Jesus produced the mystery religions, which strove for a knowledge of God through the mysteries, that were passed on only to those who had been properly initiated and sworn to secrecy. Their sects were many, their rules were strict; revelation of the mysteries to any unauthorized person was a crime the punishment for which, in some sects, was death.

Among the most important offshoots of these were the Gnostics, of whom there were many, divided into many sects.

Gnosticism was a great syncretic movement that tended to blend several religions into a world religion in which the new mystique of Jesus as the Christ could take its place along with the older faiths that had swayed the region earlier. "The Gnostics," wrote Adolf Harnack, "were the theologians of the first century; they were the first to transform Christianity into a system of doctrines; they were the first to treat tradition and the primitive Christian scriptures systematically; they undertook to set forth Christianity as the absolute religion, and therefore placed it in opposition to other religions, to that of the Old Testament as well, but the absolute religion, which they coupled with Christ, was to them essentially identical with the results of the philosophy of religion, for which they had found a new basis in a revelation. They were accordingly a class of Christians

who emerged through a sharp onset to conquer Christianity for
Hellenic culture, and Hellenic culture for Christianity. . . .
Christianity became an occult theosophy, (revealed metaphysics
and apparent philosophy) permeated with the Platonic spirit
and with Pauline ideas, constructed out of the material of an
old cultus-wisdom which was acquired through mysteries and
the illuminated understanding, defined by a keen and, in part,
true criticism of the Old Testament religion and the scant faith
of the church. Consequently one is obliged to verify the promi-
nent gnostic cosmological principles, the Hellenic philosophical
ideas, and the knowledge of the redemption of the world
through Christ."[2]

Further, in Gnostic Christian doctrine, "the good and the
heavenly which is degraded to the material, is the human spirit;
and the sublime power which sets it free, is the Christ. The
Gospel history is not the history of Christ, but a collection of
allegorical representations of the great divine world-history.
Christ has, indeed, no history; his appearance in this world of
confusion and delusion is his own act and enlightenment of the
spirit, as regards itself, is the effect of this act."[3]

The religion that sprang from the life and teachings of Jesus
and their interpretations by those who regarded him as the
Christ had in it much of the kind of mystery that appealed to
Gnosticism and so was taken over, and given its own interpretation by the Gnostics. The ethical teachings of Jesus, as passed
on by the apostles, required, in the view of the Gnostics, interpretation, for, though the literal meaning was sufficient for the
ordinary people, there was deeper meaning in them available
only to the elect through an understanding of the mysteries, an
esoteric doctrine and an inner meaning which could be imparted
to the worthy alone.

In view of this there were a number of gospels and apocalypses
—that is, writings dealing with theories concerning the end of the
world—written supposedly under the influence of the holy spirit,
all professing to be the teachings Jesus gave to his disciples
after the "resurrection from the dead"—which, in Gnostic termi-

nology, meant the new birth that was possible only through illumination given by the Gnostic mysteries. These books have made up a sizable proportion of the so-called New Testament Apocrypha.

As to the personality of the physical Jesus (distinguished in Gnostic doctrine from the divine Christ), there was every shade of opinion among the many Gnostic sects, ranging from the view that he was simply a good and holy man to that which made him "very God of very God."

The serious study of Gnosticism has been, for the most part, confined to the work of a few specialized scholars; the difficulty involved in understanding the Gnostic terminology, and the wide variety of doctrines and details in the various sects, what G. R. S. Mead has called "the indefinite chaos of the Gnostics," has made the subject one that can become only confusing to the ordinary reader or student. It thus seems hopeless to attempt anything like a definite outline of the Gnostic "system," for indeed it was not one, but many systems, each as inunderstandable as the others.

Further, G. R. S. Mead wrote, "The Gnostics were ever changing their nomenclature; the god of one system might be the devil of another. He who makes a concordance of names, merely, in Gnosticism, may think himself lucky to escape a lunatic asylum. . . . If we were to bring all these contrary accounts together and treat them to a critical analysis it is to be feared that the general reader . . . would either close our pages in despair, or, if he attempted to follow the details and the weighing of probabilities, be reduced to such a state of perturbation that he would forget all that had gone before, and be rendered totally unfit to comprehend what is to follow."⁴

Thus it is evident that any attempt to make a complete and lucid explanation of Gnosticism, or definition of its terms, is futile, and best not attempted, partly because it was not one but actually many religions, partly because the meanings of its terms were, as a rule, carefully hidden from all but the initiates, partly because so little of its actual literature is extant, and most of what is known of the various systems comes from comments by early writers who were not themselves Gnostics, but for the most part condemned the complicated systems that made up Gnosticism as heresies.

Not all of the apocryphal New Testament books came from the Gnostics by any means, though many did. Many of what might be called "orthodox" Christian sects (a term loosely used here, for orthodoxy in these early centuries of the infant Christian religion was a fairly vague term) also produced gospels, acts, epistles, and apocalypses. And, in order to give them a semblance of authenticity, the names of apostles (as, actually, in the books of the New Testament that are now a part of the orthodox Christian Bible) were given them. Some of these were used in some Christian communities, others in other communities. The New Testament Canon was slowly formed, and gradually many of the books, now considered apocryphal, some Gnostic and some not, were excluded. The list of books that now make up the accepted New Testament of the Christian Church was compiled in Rome in A.D. 382 and confirmed by the Council of Trent in the sixteenth century. Those that had been written with the same purpose as that which inspired the writing of the books in our New Testament, but not included, comprise the New Testament Apocrypha.

I hesitate to leave the discussion of Gnosticism without inserting a quotation—not from a Gnostic book, but from the letter of a leader of one Gnostic faith, an Arabian of the latter half of the second century, named Monoimus. He states in this, rather more beautifully than the same idea is propounded in other religious texts (Luke 17:21, in the King James Version of the Bible, for instance, in several places in the Upanishads, in a statement by the fourteenth-century B.C. Egyptian King Amenhotep IV, commonly known as Akhenaton, or Ikhnaton), his belief in the divinity that dwells within mankind.

"Cease to seek after God as without thee, and the universe, and things similar to these; seek Him from out of thyself, and learn who it is who once and for all appropriates all in thee himself, and say, 'My God, my mind, my soul, my body.' And learn whence is sorrow and joy, love and hate, and waking though one would not, and sleeping though one would not, and getting angry though one would not, and falling in love, though one would not. And if thou closely investigate these things thou wilt find him in thyself, one and many, thus finding from thyself a way out of thyself."[5]

Often the Gnostic doctrine was proclaimed in writings that are almost incomprehensible to any save the especially instructed, as, for example, in the extracts from the Pistis Sophia, The Book of the Savior, and The Gospel of Truth in the present volume. Others are very like the statements in the canonical gospels. A favorite mode of expression in Gnostic literature was the seeming refutation by paradox, as in the recorded appearance to John in the apocryphal Acts of John, where Jesus is reported to have said, "I suffered, yet I did not suffer; I was pierced yet I was not smitten, hanged and I was not hanged," etc.

One might speculate with interest whether, as much conventional Christian dogma entered Gnosticism, any purely Gnostic doctrine is echoed in the canonical New Testament, and one instantly thinks of Matthew 10:39, "He that findeth his life shall lose it, and he that loseth his life for my sake shall find it." If we omit the phrase "for my sake," which could well have been inserted by a redactor, we would have a typically Gnostic statement. Jesus' reported remark in Mark 4:11, "Unto you it is given to know the mystery of the kingdom of God," and similar mentions of "mysteries" in some twenty other places in the New Testament, chiefly in the Epistles, are distinctly suggestive of Gnostic influence.

Not the least interesting of the books and fragments are the heretical books, passages from some of which are still extant, such as The Gospel according to the Hebrews, quoted by Epiphanius, in which the unique divinity of Jesus is denied, saying that he was "born of the seed of a man." Thus it is obvious that, though the teaching of Paul and his followers prevailed in the firm foundation they laid for Christian Church dogma, there is evidence here that Jesus was accepted by some as a great Jewish teacher, a "rab," rather than as the "only son of God."

Another source of interest lies in the fact that, while none of the books used as sources for the present volume was ever admitted to the Canon of the Christian Church, a number of them were given credence by the early church fathers, and some dogmas and Christian Church traditions for which there is no authority in the Canon seem to have had their origins here, unless, as has been suggested, the Church traditions were established first, and came into the Apocrypha later.

And in addition their imaginative story value and their frequent mystical beauty are ample justification for the attempt made in this book, through a chronological arrangement of the material, and explanatory notes, to bring them more forcefully to public attention.

The two principal sources of the material are *The Apocryphal New Testament*, translated by Montague Rhodes James, Oxford, at the Clarendon Press, 1926, and *Fragments of a Faith Forgotten* by G. R. S. Mead (London: John M. Watkins, 1931). Other sources, not properly a part of the New Testament Apocrypha (and indeed two that are non-Christian), are identified where used.

THE OTHER JESUS

1

---◆---

THE MOTHER OF JESUS

THE BIRTH OF MARY

The familiar gospels of the New Testament, Matthew, Mark, Luke, and John, begin the story on which the faith of Christianity is founded with the birth of Jesus. But the writers of the Apocrypha, in order to establish the dogma of the immaculate conception of Mary, or, as some exegetes believe, to report a doctrine already well established, begin with the story of his grandmother and grandfather.

The Protevangelium, from which most of the following account has been taken, is also known as The Book of James, The Birth of Our Lord and Our Lady Mary, and by other titles. It purports to have been written by James, the half brother of Jesus, son of Joseph by a wife who preceded Mary. Scholarly research, however, has established convincing evidence that it could not have been written before 150, and therefore could not have been written by James. As is the case with other apocryphal books, and, for that matter, with the familiar Matthew, Mark, Luke, and John, the name of an apostle has been taken as the author to convey the impression of authority and authenticity.

There are several texts of the manuscript in existence, in several languages, some evidently as late as the sixth century, and a standard text in Greek which is a product of the sixteenth century.

The Protevangelium, as well as other so-called "infancy gospels," was probably written in an attempt to establish two

*doctrines of the infant Christian Church in opposition to ob-
jections voiced by non-believers: the birth of Jesus as a miracu-
lous appearance of special divinity on earth, and the complete
absence of original sin from and the perpetual virginity of Mary.
There were two charges against the latter statement. One was a
story circulated in the early centuries of Christianity that Jesus
was born out of wedlock, the son of Mary by a Roman soldier
named Panthera; the other was the report in the primitive
tradition that Jesus had brothers and sisters, thus denying Mary's
perpetual virginity. The Protevangelium and other infancy
gospels, if accepted as history, dispose of both of these. The
statement in the Protevangelium that Joseph had sons by an
earlier marriage, other than Jesus, was strongly attacked by
Jerome, a fourth-century biblical scholar and a papal secretary,
who stated that these were actually cousins of Jesus. This view
was adopted by the Vatican after Jerome, and became official
Roman Catholic doctrine.*

The text of the Protevangelium follows.

In the records of the twelve tribes of Israel it is recounted
that there was a man named Joachim, who, being very rich,
made double offering unto the Lord, saying, "My substance
shall be for the whole people, and that I may receive mercy
from the Lord God, and forgiveness for my sins."

But at a certain great feast of the Lord, when the children of
Israel offered their gifts, and Joachim also offered his, Reuben,
the high priest, opposed him, saying, "It is not lawful for thee to
offer thy gifts, seeing thou hast begotten no issue in Israel."

And Joachim, who was greatly grieved, went away and consulted the registries of the twelve tribes, to see whether there
were not others who had begotten no seed. But he found that all
the righteous had raised up seed.

Then he remembered how God, in the latter days of Abraham's life, had given him the son Isaac, and, greatly saddened,
he went into the wilderness and pitched his tent there, and
fasted forty days and forty nights, saying, "I will not go down

to eat or drink till the Lord, my God, shall look down upon me and my prayer shall be my meat and drink."

And while he was gone his wife Anna grieved doubly, saying, "I will mourn both my widowhood and my childlessness."

On the day of a great feast unto the Lord, Judith, her maid, spoke unto her.

"How long wilt thou thus afflict thy soul?" she asked. "The feast of the Lord is now come, when it is unlawful for any one to mourn. Therefore take this headband which is fit for royalty, and which was given to me who am unfit to wear it, being a handmaid."

But Anna said unto her, "This is not for me whom the Lord hath greatly humbled. Has some evil person given thee this that thou art come to pollute me with thy sin?"

Then Judith, her maid, answered her, "What evil should I wish thee when thou wilt not hearken unto me? I could not wish you a greater sorrow than that which you now bear, in that God hath shut up your womb that you may not be a mother in Israel."

At this Anna was exceedingly troubled, and, having put off her mourning garments put on those she had worn as a bride and walked in her garden. And she saw a laurel tree and sat under it, praying to the Lord: "O, God of my fathers, bless me and regard my prayer as thous didst bless Sarah, and gavest her a son, Isaac."

And as she was looking toward heaven she saw a sparrow's nest in the laurel. And she mourned, and said:

"Woe is me; who begat me? And what womb bore me that I should thus be accursed before the Children of Israel, and that they should reproach and deride me in the temple of my God?

"Woe is me! To what may I be compared? I cannot be likened to the very beasts of the earth, for they are fruitful before thee, O Lord!

"Woe is me! To what may I be compared?

"I cannot be compared to the waters, for even the waters are fruitful before thee, O Lord!

"Woe is me! To what may I be compared?"

And lo, an angel of the Lord came and stood beside Anna and said, "Anna, Anna, the Lord hath heard thy prayer; thou shalt conceive and bear a child, and lo, it shall be spoken of in the whole world."

And Anna answered, "As the Lord, my God, liveth, whatever I bring forth, whether it be male or female, I shall devote it to the Lord my God, and it shall minister to him all the days of its life."

And there came two others saying unto her, "Behold Joachim, thy husband, comes with his sheep! For an angel of the Lord hath also come to him and said, 'The Lord God hath heard thy prayer, make haste and go thence, for behold thy wife Anna shall conceive.'"

And Joachim went down and called his shepherds, saying, "Bring me hither ten she-lambs without spot or blemish, and they shall be for the Lord my God. And bring me twelve calves without blemish, and the twelve calves shall be for the priests and elders. Bring me also an hundred goats, and the hundred goats shall be for the whole people."

And Joachim went down with the shepherds, and Anna stood by the gate and saw Joachim coming with the shepherds. And she ran, and, hanging about his neck, said, "Now I know that the Lord hath greatly blessed me; for behold I, who was a widow, am no longer a widow, and I, who was barren, shall conceive."

Now Joachim abode the first day in his house, but on the morrow he brought his offerings and said, "If the Lord be propitious to me let the plate which is on the priest's forehead make it manifest." [See Exodus 28:36.]

And after he had made his offering he looked upon the plate which the priest wore, and saw that no sin was found in him. So he went down from the temple of the Lord justified, and returned to his own house.

When her nine months were fulfilled to Anna, she brought

forth, and said to the midwife, "What have I brought forth?"
And the midwife told her, "A girl."

And Anna said, "The Lord hath this day magnified my soul,"
and she rested.

And when the days of her purification were accomplished
she gave suck to the child and called her name Mary.[1]

THE CHILDHOOD OF THE MOTHER OF JESUS

*The narrative continues in the Protevangelium logically with
an account of the childhood of Mary.*

And the child increased in strength every day, so that when
she was nine months old her mother put her upon the ground
to try if she could stand; and when she had walked nine steps,
she came again to her mother.

Then her mother caught her up and said, "As my Lord
liveth, thou shalt not walk again on this earth till I bring thee
into the temple of the Lord."

And she purified her chamber, and suffered nothing unclean
to come near her, and she called for the pure and undefiled
daughters of Israel to come and attend the child.

Now when Mary was a year old Joachim made a great
feast and invited the priests, the scribes, the elders, and all
the people of Israel. And he brought Mary to the priests, who
blessed her, saying, "The God of our fathers bless this girl,
and make her famous throughout all generations." And all the
people replied, "Amen."

And once more Joachim took the girl to the priests and they
blessed her, saying, "O most high God, regard this girl and
bless her with an everlasting blessing."

At this her mother took her up and gave her the breast, and
sang the following song to the Lord:
"*I will sing a new song unto the Lord, my God,
For he hath visited me*

And taken away from me the reproach of mine enemies,
And hath given me the fruit of his righteousness,
That it may now be told to Israel
That Anna giveth suck."

Then she put the child to rest in the room that she had consecrated, and she went out and ministered unto them. And when the feast was over they went away rejoicing and praising the God of Israel.

Now when the girl was two years old, Joachim said to Anna, "Let us take her to the temple of the Lord, that we may perform our vow, lest God should be angry with us and consider our offering unacceptable."

But Anna said, "Let us wait until the third year has passed, lest the child should grieve for her mother and her father." And Joachim said, "Let us wait."

When the child was three years old Joachim said, "Let us invite the daughters of Israel who are undefiled, and let each of them take a lighted lamp, that the child may not turn back again, and her mind be set against the temple of the Lord."

And they did this, and ascended into the temple. And the high priest received the child and blessed her, saying, "Mary, the Lord God hath magnified thy name to all generations, and to the very end of time the Lord will show his redemption to the children of Israel, through thee."

And he placed her on the third step of the altar, and the Lord gave her grace, and she danced with her feet, and all the house of Israel loved her.

And Mary continued in the temple as a dove, and received her food from the hand of an angel.[2]

THE MARRIAGE OF MARY AND JOSEPH

The close association between Jesus and John the Baptist seems to be foreshadowed in this early episode, in which the high priest Zacharias plays a part, for Zacharias was the father of

*John the Baptist, and the husband of Elizabeth, who is re-
ported to have been the cousin of Mary.*

And when she was twelve years of age the priests met in
a council, saying, "Behold Mary is twelve years old in the
temple of the Lord. What shall we do with her for fear lest
the holy place of the Lord our God should be defiled?"

Then they said to the high priest, "Stand thou at the altar of
the Lord. Enter in and petition concerning her, and whatever
the Lord shall make manifest to thee, that let us do."

So the high priest took the breast-plate of judgement and
went in unto the Holy of Holies and prayed concerning her.
And behold the angel of the Lord appeared saying unto him,
"Zacharias, Zacharias, go forth and call together all the widowers
of the people, and let them bring every man a rod, and to
whomsoever the Lord shall show a sign, his wife shall she be."

And the criers went out through all Judaea, and the trumpet
of the Lord sounded, and all the people ran and met together.
And Joseph cast down his hatchet and ran to meet them, and
when they were gathered they went to the high priest and
took their rods with them. And he took the rods of them all
and went into the temple and prayed. When he had finished
the prayer, he took the rods back and went forth and gave
them back to them, and no miracle attended them.

The last rod was Joseph's, and lo, a dove came forth of the
rod and flew upon his head. And the high priest said, "Unto
thee hath it fallen to take the virgin of the Lord and keep her
for thyself."

But Joseph refused, saying, "I am an old man and have
children, but she is a young girl; and I fear lest I become
ridiculous in Israel."

Then the priest said unto Joseph, "Fear the Lord, thy God,
and remember what things God did to Dathan and Abiram
and Korah [see Numbers 16:1–35], and how the earth clave and
they were swallowed up because of their disobedience. And
now, fear thou, Joseph, lest it happen this way with thee."

Joseph then became afraid and took her unto his house. And he said unto Mary, "Lo, I have received thee out of the temple of the Lord, and now do I leave thee in my house and I go away to build my buildings, and I will come again unto thee. The Lord shall watch over thee."[3]

". . . CONCEIVED BY THE HOLY GHOST . . ."

There are several versions of the story which apparently is the source of the "Hail Mary" ritual. One of these, from the Protevangelium, follows.

Now there was a council of the priests, and they said, "Let us make a veil for the temple of the Lord." And the priest said, "Call together seven undefiled virgins of the tribe of David." And messages went out and sought and found them and brought them to the temple of the Lord. And the priests called to mind the child Mary, that was of the tribe of David and was undefiled before God, and the officers went and fetched her.

And the high priest said, "Cast lots before me now, who of you shall spin the gold, and the undefiled (the white), and the fine linen, and the silk, and the hyacinthine, and the scarlet, and the true purple." And the scarlet fell unto Mary, and she went away to her house.

From that time Zacharias, the high priest, became dumb, and Samuel was in his place until the time when Zacharias spoke again.

And Mary took the scarlet and began to spin it.

And she took a pot and went forth to fill it with water, and heard a voice saying, "Hail thou that art highly favored; the Lord is with thee; blessed art thou among women."

And she looked about her to the right and to the left, to see whence this voice came, and, trembling, went into her house and set down the water pot, and took the scarlet and sat down upon her seat and began to work it.

And behold the angel of the Lord stood before her, saying,

"Fear not, Mary, for thou hast found favor in the sight of God. The Lord is with thee and thou shalt conceive."

And she, when she heard it, questioned herself, saying, "Shall I verily conceive of the living God, and bring forth as all other women do?"

But the angel of the Lord said, "Not so, Mary, for a power of the Lord shall overshadow thee: wherefore that which shall be born of thee shall be most holy, and shall be called the Son of the Living God. And thou shalt call his name Jesus, for he shall save his people from their sins."*

And Mary said, "Behold the handmaid of the Lord is before him. Be it unto me according to thy word."[4]

There is another account of the annunciation to Mary in The Gospel of Bartholomew, in which the story is told in the first person by Mary years later, after the crucifixion and resurrection of Jesus. The work was mentioned by several of the early Church Fathers and is one of several texts associated with the name of the apostle; they exist in Greek, Latin, Slavonic, and Coptic. The Coptic version is at least as late as the fifth century, and shows distinct Gnostic tendencies. The original form of The Gospel of Bartholomew, however, seems to have appeared in the third century. The story of Mary's experience in the temple at the time of the annunciation which follows is but a small part of the gospel, other parts of which appear in different contexts in this book. The identity of the "John" in the following account, among the several Johns mentioned in the Bible, is established by the first sentence in the selection that follows, as the apostle John, known during the early years of Jesus' ministry as "the beloved disciple."

Now the apostles were with Mary. And Bartholomew came and said unto Peter and Andrew and John, "Let us ask her that is highly favored how she conceived the incomprehensible, or

---

* "Jesus" is the Greek form of the Hebrew "Joshua," which means literally, "Jehovah saves."

how she bare him that cannot be carried, or how she brought forth so much greatness."

But they doubted to ask her.

Bartholomew therefore said unto Peter, "Thou that art the chief, and my teacher, draw near and ask her."

But Peter said to John, "Thou art a virgin and undefiled, and thou must ask her."

And as they all doubted and disputed, Bartholomew came near unto her with a cheerful countenance and said to her, "Thou that art highly favored, the tabernacle of the Most High, unblemished, we, even all the apostles, ask thee to tell us how thou didst conceive the incomprehensible, or how thou didst bear him that cannot be carried, or how thou didst bring forth so much greatness."

But Mary said unto them, "Ask me not concerning this mystery. If I should begin to tell you fire would issue out of my mouth and consume all the world."

But they continued yet the more to ask her. And she, for she could not refuse to hear the apostles, said, "Let us stand up in prayer."

And the apostles stood behind Mary, but she said unto Peter, "Peter, thou chief, thou great pillar, standest thou behind us? Said not the Lord, 'The head of man is Christ'? Now therefore stand ye before me and pray."

But they said unto her, "In thee did the Lord set his tabernacle, and it was his good pleasure that thou shouldest contain him, and thou oughtest to be the leader in the prayer."

But she said unto them, "Ye are shining stars, and as the prophet said, 'I did lift up mine eyes unto the hills, from whence shall come mine help' [Psalm 121], ye, therefore, are the hills, and it behoveth you to pray."

The apostles say unto her, "Thou oughtest to pray, thou art the mother of the heavenly king."

Mary saith unto them, "In your likeness did God form the sparrows, and sent them forth into the four corners of the world."

But they say unto her, "He that is scarce contained by the seven heavens was pleased to be contained in thee."

Then Mary stood before them and spread out her hands toward the heaven and began to speak thus: "O God, the exceeding great and all-wise and king of the worlds, that art not to be described, the ineffable, that did establish the greatness of the heavens and all things by a word, that out of darkness didst constitute and fasten together the poles of heaven in harmony, didst bring into shape matter that was in confusion, didst bring into order the things that were without order, didst part the misty darkness from the light, didst establish in one place the foundations of the waters, thou that makest the beings of the earth to tremble, and art the fear of them that are on the earth, that didst settle the earth and not suffer it to perish, and filldst it, which is the nourisher of all things, with showers of blessings, son of the father, thou whom the seven heavens hardly contained, but who was well pleased to be contained without pain in me, thou that art thyself the full word of the Father in whom all things came to be; give glory to thy great name, and bid me to speak before thy holy apostles."

And when she had ended the prayer she said unto them, "Let us sit upon the ground, and come thou, Peter, the chief, and sit on my right hand and put thy left hand beneath mine armpit, and thou, Andrew, do so on my left hand, and thou, John, the virgin, hold together my bosom, and thou, Bartholomew, set thy knees against my back and hold my shoulders, lest when I begin to speak my bones be loosed one from another."

And when they had done so, she said, "When I abode in the temple of God and received my food from an angel, on a certain day there appeared unto me one in the likeness of an angel, but his face was incomprehensible, and he had not in the hand bread or a cup, as did the angel that came to me aforetime. And straightway the veil of the temple was rent and there was a very great earthquake, and I fell upon the earth, for I was not able to endure the sight of him. But he put his hand beneath me and raised me up, and I looked up into heaven and there came a cloud of dew and sprinkled me from the head to the feet, and he wiped me with his robe.

"And he said unto me, 'Hail, thou that art highly favored, the chosen vessel, grace inexhaustible.' And he smote his garment upon the right hand and there came a very great loaf, and he set it upon the altar of the temple and did eat of it first himself, and gave unto me also. And again he smote his garment upon the left hand, and there came a very great cup of wine; and he set it upon the altar of the temple and did drink of it first himself, and gave unto me also. And I beheld and saw the bread and the cup whole, as they were.

"'Yet three years and I will send my word unto thee and thou shalt conceive my son, and through him shall the whole creation be saved. Peace be unto thee, my beloved, and my peace shall be with thee continually.'

"And when he had said so he vanished from mine eyes, and the temple was restored as it had been before."[5]

The story of Mary is continued in the Protevangelium.

And when she [Mary] had wrought the purple and the scarlet, she carried them unto the priest. And the priest blessed her and said, "Mary, the Lord God hath magnified thy name and thou shalt be blessed among all generations of the earth."

And Mary, filled with joy, went away unto Elizabeth her kinswoman, and knocked at the door. And when Elizabeth heard, she ran and opened to her, and when she saw Mary she blessed her and said, "Whence is this to me that the mother of my Lord should come unto me? For behold that which is in me leaped and blessed thee."*

And Mary forgot the mysteries which the Angel had told her, and she looked up to heaven and said, "Who am I, Lord, that all the generations of the earth do bless me?"

And she abode three months with Elizabeth and day by

---

* Elizabeth was at this time pregnant with a son, who was to be John the Baptist.

day her womb grew and Mary was afraid and departed unto her house and hid herself from the children of Israel. Now she was sixteen years old when these mysteries came to pass.[6]

THE TEST

In the familiar gospels according to Matthew, Mark, Luke, and John, Joseph is satisfied with the explanation of the angel that Mary is to bear a child conceived by the Holy Ghost, but in the apocryphal Protevangelium the matter becomes one for the priests to settle and both Mary and Joseph are made to drink the "water of conviction," as described in the book of Numbers. The concoction was composed of holy water and sweepings from the floor of the tabernacle. If those who drank it became ill they were judged guilty; if not, innocent.

And when her sixth month had come, Joseph returned from his building, and he entered into his house and found her great with child. Then, smiting his face, he cried bitterly, saying, "With what countenance can I look upon the Lord, my God? And what shall I say concerning this young woman? For I received her a virgin out of the temple of the Lord my God, and have not preserved her as such. Who is he that hath deceived me? Who hath done this evil in mine house and hath defiled the virgin? Is not the history of Adam accomplished in me? For in the instant of his glory the serpent came and found Eve alone and deceived her. So hath it befallen me."

Then Joseph called Mary, and said unto her, "Oh thou that hast been favored by God, why hast thou done this? Why hast thou debased thy soul, thou that wast educated in the Holy of Holies, and didst receive food at the hand of angels?"

But she wept, saying, "I am innocent and have known no man."

And Joseph said unto her, "How then is it that thou art with child?"

And she said, "As the Lord my God liveth, I know not by what means."

And Joseph was exceedingly afraid, and went away from her, and wondered what he should do with her, and reasoned, "If I hide her sin I shall be found guilty of opposing the law of the Lord, and if I exhibit her unto the children of Israel, I fear lest, if she is with child by an angel, I shall be found to betray the life of an innocent person. What, then, shall I do? I will privately dismiss her."

Then the night was come upon him, when behold, an angel of the Lord appeared to him in a dream, and said, "Fear not, for what which is in the young woman is of the Holy Ghost, and she shall bring forth a son, and thou shalt call his name Jesus, for he shall save his people from their sins."

Then Joseph arose from his sleep and glorified the God of Israel who had shown him such favor, and preserved the virgin.

Then came Annas, the scribe, and said to him, "Wherefore have we not seen you since your return?"

And Joseph replied, "Because I was weary with the journey, and I rested the first day."

And Annas turned him about, and saw Mary, great with child. And he went away to the priest, and said unto him, "Joseph, in whom you placed so much confidence, hath sinned grievously, in that he hath defiled the virgin whom he received out of the temple of the Lord, and hath secretly married her."

And the priest said, "Hath Joseph done this?"

And Annas said, "If you will send servants you will find that she is with child."

And the servants went and found as he had said, and they brought her together with Joseph, unto the place of judgement. . . .

And the priest said unto Mary, "What hast thou done?"

And Mary, weeping, answered, "As the Lord my God liveth, I am innocent in his sight, seeing I have known no man."

And the priest said, "I will cause you both to drink of the

water of the conviction of the Lord, and it will make manifest your sins before your eyes." [See Numbers 5:12–28.]

And the priest took the water, and made Joseph drink and sent him into the hill country. And he returned whole. He made Mary drink also, and sent her into the hill country. And she returned whole. And all the people marvelled because sin appeared not in them.

And the priest said, "Since the Lord hath not made your sin evident, neither do I condemn thee."

So he sent them away. And Joseph took Mary and departed unto his house rejoicing, and glorifying the God of Israel.[7]

2

THE CHILDHOOD OF JESUS

"... BORN OF THE VIRGIN MARY ..."

In the following, that portion of the narrative which is told by Joseph in the first person is believed by scholars to be an insertion from another manuscript. If this is the case, however, it has not been identified.

And it came to pass that there went out a decree from the Emperor Augustus the king that all the Jews should be taxed who were of Bethlehem of Judaea. And Joseph said, "I will take care that my sons obey, but what shall I do with this young woman? How shall I record her? As my wife? Nay, I am ashamed. Or as my daughter? But all the children of Israel know that she is not my daughter. Let the Lord do as seems good to him."

And he saddled his ass, and put her upon it, and Joseph followed after. And they drew within three miles of Bethlehem. Then Joseph . . . saw Mary sorrowful and said within himself, "Perhaps she is in pain because of that which is within her." But when he turned again he saw her laughing, and said unto her, "Mary, why is it that I see thy face at one time laughing and at another time sad?"

And Mary replied, "I see two people with mine eyes, the one weeping and mourning, and the other laughing and rejoicing."

And Mary said unto him, "Take me down from the ass, for that which is within me presses to come forth."

But Joseph said, "Whither shall I take thee? . . . for the place is a desert."

And he found a cave there and brought her into it, and set his sons by her, and he went forth and sought for a midwife of the Hebrews in the country of Bethlehem.

Now I, Joseph, looked up to the air and saw the air and saw the clouds astonished, and the fowls of the air without motion. And I looked upon the earth and saw a table spread and workmen sitting around it, and their hands were upon the table and they did not move to eat. But all of them were looking upward. And I beheld sheep being driven, yet the sheep stood still; and the shepherd lifted his hand to smite them with his staff, and his hand remained up. And I looked upon a river and saw the kids with their mouths upon the water, and they drank not.

Then I beheld a woman coming down from the mountains, and she said to me, "Man, whither goest thou?"

I said, "I go to inquire for a Hebrew midwife."

She answered and said unto me, "Art thou of Israel?"

I said to her, "Yea."

And she said, "Where is the woman that is to be delivered?"

And I answered, "In the cave. It is she that is betrothed to me."

"Is she not thy wife?"

"It is Mary that was educated in the house of the Lord, and she fell to my lot, and is not my wife, but she hath conceived by the Holy Ghost."

The narrative now returns to the third person.

And the midwife said unto him, "Is this true?"

And Joseph said unto her, "Come and see."

And they stood in the place of the cave, and a bright cloud overshadowed the cave. And the midwife said, "My soul is magnified this day because mine eyes have seen marvelous things; for salvation is born unto Israel."

And on a sudden the cloud became a great light in the cave so that the eyes could not endure it. But the light gradually decreased until the young child appeared and took the breast of its mother, Mary.

And the midwife cried aloud and said, "Great unto me today is this day, in that I have seen this extraordinary sight."

And the midwife went out of the cave and Salome met her. And the midwife said, "Salome, a new sight have I to tell thee. A virgin hath brought forth, which is a thing contrary to nature."

And Salome said, "As the Lord my God liveth, unless I receive proof I shall not believe that a virgin hath brought forth."

And the midwife went in and said unto Mary, "Order thyself, for a great controversy is arisen concerning thee."

Then Salome received satisfaction. But her hand was withered and she cried out, "Woe unto mine iniquity, for I have tempted the living God, and my hand is ready to drop off."

And she made supplication unto the Lord, saying, "O God of my fathers, remember me, for I am the seed of Abraham and Isaac and Jacob; make me not a reproach among the children of Israel, but restore me, for thou knowest, Lord, that in thy name did I perform my cures, and did receive my reward from thee."

And an angel of the Lord stood by Salome and said, "The Lord God hath heard thy prayer; reach forth thy hand unto the young child and take him up, and thou shalt be restored."

And Salome came near and took him up, saying, "I will do him worship, for a great king is born unto Israel."

And straightway Salome was cured and she went forth of the cave. And lo, a voice, saying, "Salome, Salome, tell none of the marvels which thou hast seen until the child enter Jerusalem."[1]

THE MIDWIFE'S ACCOUNT

The Arundel Manuscript, from which the following account is taken, a fourteenth-century document in the British Museum, purports to have been written from information given by

Symeon, a son of Joseph. The truth, however, is that it is
probably a combination of material taken from the Protevan-
gelium and The Gospel of Pseudo-Matthew. The actual author
is, of course, unknown.

When therefore the hour drew nearer, the might of God
manifested itself. And the maiden (Mary) stood looking up to
heaven, and became snow white. For now the end of the
events of salvation was far advanced. And when the light had
come forth, Mary worshipped him whom she saw that she had
brought forth. And the child himself shone brightly round
about like the sun, and was pure and most beautiful to behold,
since he alone appeared as peace spreading peace everywhere.
And in that hour when he was born there was heard a voice
of many invisible beings saying with one accord "Amen." And
the light itself which was born increased and darkened the
light of the sun with the brightness of its shining. And this
cave was filled with bright light together with a most sweet
odour. This light was born just as dew descends on the earth
from heaven. For its odour is more fragrant than any aroma
of ointments.

And I stood there stupefied and amazed, and fear seized me.
For I was looking upon the intense brightness of the light
which was born. But the light itself, gradually withdrawing,
became like a child, and in a moment became a child as
children are customarily born. And I took courage and bent
down and touched him, and took him up in my hands with
great fear, and was seized with terror because he had no
weight like other children who are born. And I looked at him
and there was no defilement in him, but he was in all his body
shining as in the dew of the most high God, light to carry,
radiant to behold. And while I wondered greatly because he
did not cry as new-born babes are accustomed to cry, and
while I held him and looked at his face, he smiled at me
with the most sweet smile, and opened his eyes and looked

sharply on me. And suddenly there came forth from his eyes a great light like a brilliant flash of lightning.[2]

THE MURDEROUS ANGER OF HEROD

And behold Joseph made him ready to go away. And there came great disorder in Bethlehem of Judaea for there came wise men, saying, "Where is the king of the Jews born? For we have seen his star in the East and are come to worship him."

When Herod heard this he was exceedingly troubled and sent messengers unto the wise men, and to the high priests and examined them, saying, "Where have you written concerning the Christ, or where should he be born?"

They say unto him, "In Bethlehem of Judaea, for thus it is written."

And having sent away the priests he inquired of the wise men, saying, "What sign saw ye concerning the king that is born?"

They answered him, "We saw an extraordinarily large star shining among the stars of heaven, and so outshining all the other stars that they appeared not, and thereby knew that a great king was born to Israel and came to worship him."

Herod said, "Go and seek for him, and if ye find him, tell me, that I may come and worship him also."

So the wise men went forth. And behold, the star which they saw in the east went before them until it stood over the cave. And the wise men saw the young child with Mary, his mother, and they brought forth out of their treasures and gave him gold and frankincense and myrrh. And, being warned in a dream by an angel that they should not enter unto Judaea, they went into their own country by another way.

Then Herod, perceiving that he was mocked by the wise men, and being very angry commanded certain men to go and kill all the children that were in Bethlehem from two years old and under.

But Mary, hearing that the children were being slain, was
afraid, and took the young child and wrapped him in swaddling
clothes, and laid him in an ox-manger because there was no
room at the inn. Elizabeth, also, when she heard that they
sought for John, took him and went up into the mountains and
looked around for a place to hide him, and there was no secret
place. And she groaned within herself, and said, "O mountain
of God, receive thee a mother with the child." For she could
not climb up. And instantly the mountain was divided and
received them. And an angel of the Lord was with them, to
preserve them.

But Herod sought for John and sent officers to Zacharias
saying, "Where hast thou hidden thy son?"

And he answered and said unto them, "I am a minister of
God and a servant at the altar. How should I know where my
son is?"

And the officers departed and told Herod all these things.
And Herod was wroth and said, "Is not his son like to be king
over Israel?" And he sent unto him again saying, "Say the
truth; where is thy son? For thou knowest that your life is in
my hand."

And the officers departed and told him all these things.

And Zacharias said, "I am a martyr of God if thou sheddest my
blood; the Lord will receive my soul. Besides, know that thou
sheddest innocent blood."

And Zacharias was murdered.[3]

THE FLIGHT INTO EGYPT

*The Gospel of Thomas, from which the following account is
taken, occurs in several texts and in parts found at different
times and different places. Indeed the different bits of manuscript that have been found under this title may be parts of
different works by different persons. The account used here is
from a Latin text apparently of the third century A.D. The
Arabic Gospel of the Infancy, cited in the following narrative,*

of unknown origin, was first translated in the seventeenth century.

When there was a tumult because search was made by Herod for our Lord Jesus Christ, that he might slay him, then said an angel unto Joseph, "Take Mary and her child and flee into Egypt from the face of them that seek to slay him."

Now Jesus was two years old when he entered into Egypt. And as he walked through a sown field he put forth his hand and took of the ears and put them upon the fire and ground them and began to eat. (And he gave such favor unto that field that year by year when it was sown it yielded unto the lord of it so many measures of wheat as the number of grains which he had taken from it.)[4]

They came to a cave and wished to rest there. Mary dismounted and sat with Jesus in her lap. . . . Suddenly a number of dragons came out of the cave and cried out with fear. Jesus got down from his mother's lap and stood before the dragons, which worshipped him. Thus was fulfilled the word, "Praise the Lord from the earth, ye dragons and all deeps." [Psalm 148.] Jesus walked before them and bade them hurt no one.

Mary was alarmed for him, but he said, "Fear not, neither conceive that I am a child, for I always was and am a perfect man, and it is necessary that all the beasts of the forest should grow tame before me."

In like manner lions and leopards adored him and accompanied them and showed them the way, and bowed their heads to Jesus. At first Mary was afraid, but Jesus smiled on her and reassured her. The lions never injured their oxen and asses or the sheep they had brought from Judaea. Wolves, too, came and were harmless. Thus they fulfilled the word, "the wolves shall feed with the lambs, the lion and the ox shall eat straw together." [Isaiah 11:6-7.]

On the third day Mary saw a palm and wished to rest under it. When she was seated she saw fruit on it and said to Joseph that she would like to have some. Joseph said he was surprised

that she should say so because the tree was so high; he himself
was thinking about water because they had so little left. Jesus,
sitting on his mother's lap, bade the palm give his mother some
of its fruit. The tree bent as low as her feet and she gathered
what she would.* He bade it rise again and give them of the
water concealed below its roots. A spring came forth and all
rejoiced and drank from it.

The next day when they left the place, Jesus said to the palm,
"I give thee this privilege, that one of thy branches shall be
taken by my angels and planted in my Father's garden. And
henceforth all who win contests shall be told that they have
won the palm of victory." An angel came and took a branch
and flew away with it. All fell down in fear, but Jesus reassured them. . . .[5]

Think that to be true which is told, that he [Jesus] was
captured by robbers in the way [during the flight into Egypt]
and saved by the kindness of a youth. This was, they say,
the son of the chief of the robbers, and when he got possession
of his prey, and found the child on his mother's breast, such
splendor of majesty appeared in his lovely face that the
youth, not doubting that he was more than man, inflamed with
love, embraced him and said, "O most blessed of children, if
ever there come a time for having mercy on me, then remember
me and forget not this hour."

This, they say, was the robber who was crucified on Christ's
right hand and, when the other blasphemed, said, "Dost thou
not fear God?" [Luke 23:40] and turning to the Lord and
beholding him in that majesty which he had seen in him as a
child, and not forgetful of his pact, said, "Remember me when
thou comest into thy kingdom."[6]

They arrived at Hermopolis and entered a city called Sotinen
and had to lodge at a temple where there were 365 gods.
When Mary and the child entered all the idols fell, and Isaiah's

---

* There is an old song, probably of Elizabethan English origin, sung in
the Kentucky mountains, about this legend, save that in the song the tree
is a cherry, rather than a date, tree. —Ed.

words were fulfilled: "Behold the Lord shall come upon a light cloud and enter Egypt, and all the gods made by the hand of the Egyptians shall be moved before his face."*

Affrodosios, governor of the city, heard of it and came with all his host. The priests thought he would punish those who had destroyed the gods, but when he saw them fallen he adored the child and said to those present, that "unless this were the God of our gods they would not have fallen. If we do not adore him, as they have done, we are in danger of such destruction as fell upon Pharaoh who was drowned with all his army."

Then all the people of the city believed in the Lord through Jesus Christ.[7]

Mary used to take hold of his hand and lead him along the roads, saying, "My sweet son, walk a little way," in the same manner as other babes are taught to walk. And he, Jesus, the very God, followed her untroubled. He clung to her with his little fingers, he stopped from time to time, and he clung to the skirts of Mary his mother, he upon whom all the universe hangeth. He would lift up his eyes to her face, and she would catch him up to herself and lift him up in her arms, and walk along with him.[8]

And as Jesus walked with Mary his mother through the midst of the market place of the city, he looked about and saw a master teaching his pupils. And behold twelve sparrows which were quarrelling one with another fell from a wall into the lap of the master who taught the boys. And when Jesus saw it he laughed and stood still.

Now, when that teacher saw him laughing, he said to his pupils in great anger, "Go bring him hither unto me."

And when they had brought him the master took him hold on his ear and said, "What sawest thou that thou didst laugh?"

And he said unto him, "Master, see my hand is full of corn,

* "Behold the LORD rideth upon a swift cloud, and shall come into Egypt: and the idols of Egypt shall be moved at his presence, and the heart of Egypt shall melt in the midst of it." (Isaiah 19:1.)

and I showed it to them and scattered the corn . . . for this cause they fought with one another that they might partake of the corn." And Jesus left not the place until it was accomplished. And for this cause the master labored to cast him out of the city together with his mother.

And behold an angel of the Lord met with Mary and said unto her, "Take the child and return into the land of the Jews; for they are dead which sought his life."

So Mary arose with Jesus, and they went into the city of Nazareth, which is in the inheritance of his father.[9]

THE CHILD WHO WORKED MIRACLES

The Gospel of Pseudo-Matthew, from which some of the following narrative is taken, is, as is true of so many apocryphal manuscripts, of uncertain origin, though a large number of manuscripts of it exist. The version from which the selection here used was taken is probably of the eighth or ninth century.

Now when Jesus was five years old there was a great rain and the child Jesus walked about therein. And the rain was very terrible; and he gathered the water into a pool and commanded with a word that it should become clear, and forthwith it did so. And he took of the clay which came of that pool and made thereof twelve sparrows.

Now it was the sabbath day when Jesus did this among the children of the Hebrews, and the children of the Hebrews went and said unto Joseph, his father, "Lo, thy son was playing with us and he took clay and made sparrows which it was not right to do upon the sabbath, and he hath broken it."

And Joseph went to the child Jesus and said, "Wherefore hast thou done this which it was not right to do on the sabbath?"

But Jesus spread forth his hands and commanded the sparrows, saying, "Go forth into the height and fly. Ye shall not meet death at any man's hands."

And they flew and began to cry out and praise almighty God.

When the Jews saw what was done they marvelled and departed, proclaiming the signs which Jesus did.

On a day when Jesus climbed up upon a house with the children he began to play with them. But one of the boys fell down through the door out of the upper chamber and died straightway. And when the children saw it they fled all of them, but Jesus remained alone in the house. And the parents of the child which had died came and spake against Jesus, saying, "Of a truth thou madest him fall."

But Jesus said, "I never made him fall," and came down from the house and stood over the dead child and cried with a loud voice, calling him by name, "Zeno, Zeno, arise and say if I made thee fall."

And on a sudden he arose and said, "Nay, Lord."

When his parents saw this great miracle which Jesus did, they glorified God and worshipped Jesus.

A certain boy of the village was cleaving wood and smote his foot. And when much people was come unto him Jesus also came with them. And he touched the foot which was hurt, and forthwith it was made whole. And Jesus said unto him, "Arise and cleave the wood and remember me." When the multitude that were with him saw the signs which were done they worshipped Jesus and said, "Of a truth we believe surely thou art God."

When it was seed time Joseph went forth to sow corn, and Jesus followed after him. When Joseph began to sow Jesus took of the corn as much as he could hold in his hand and scattered it. Joseph then came at the time of harvest to reap it. And Jesus also came and gathered the ears which he had sown, and they made an hundred measures of good corn, and he called the poor and the widows and fatherless and gave them the corn he had gained, save that Joseph took a little thereof unto his house for a blessing.

Joseph was a builder and wrought plows and yokes for oxen. And on a day a certain rich man said unto him, "Sir, make me

a bed, serviceable and comely." But Joseph was troubled
because the beam he had made ready for the work was short.

Jesus said unto him, "Be not troubled, but take hold of the
beam by the one end and I by the other, and let us draw it
out."

And so it came to pass, and forthwith Joseph found it serviceable, and embraced him, and said, "Blessed am I for that God
hath given me such a son."

Joseph sent James to gather straw, and Jesus followed after
him. And as James gathered the straw a viper bit him and
he fell to the earth as dead by means of the venom. But when
Jesus saw that, he breathed upon the wound and forthwith
James was made whole and the viper died.[10]

There is a road from Jericho to Jordan, at the place where
Israel crossed and the ark rested. Jesus, eight years old, went
from Jericho to Jordan. On the way there was a vault where was
a lioness with whelps. He went in and sat there and the whelps
played about him; the older lions stood at a distance and
adored him, wagging their tails. The people who saw it said
that he or his parents must have sinned or he would not have
delivered himself to the lions. Then he came forth, and the
lions went before him, and the whelps played before his feet.
His parents and the people looked on. Jesus said, "How much
better than you are the beasts which know me and are tame,
while ye know me not."[11]

Joseph came to a feast with his sons, Joseph, Juda, and
Simeon, and his two daughters. Jesus and Mary came with her
sister Mary of Cleophas, whom the Lord gave to her father
and her mother, because they had offered Mary to the Lord
and this other was given for their consolation and called by
the same name. When they were together Jesus blessed and
sanctified them, and was the first to eat and drink, for no one
ventured even to sit down until he had done so, and all
waited for him if he was not there. And his brethren watched
him ever and feared him, and the light of God shone always
over him.[12]

They went into a city where there was a woman possessed
with a devil, and in whom Satan, that cursed rebel, had taken
up his abode. One night, when she went to fetch water, she
could neither endure her clothes on, nor to be in any house;
but as often as they tied her with chains or cords, she brake
them, and went out into desert places, and sometimes standing
where roads crossed, and in churchyards, would throw stones
at men.

When Mary saw this woman, she pitied her; whereupon
Satan presently left her, and fled her, and fled away in the
form of a young man, saying, "Woe to me, because of thee,
Mary, and thy son."

So the woman was delivered from her torment; but con-
sidering herself naked, she blushed, and avoided seeing any
man, and having put on her clothes, went home, and gave
an account of her case to her father and relations, who, as they
were the best of the city, entertained Mary and Joseph with
the greatest respect.

The next morning having received a sufficient supply of
provisions for the road, they went from them, and about the
evening of the day arrived at another town, where a marriage
was then about to be solemnized; but by the arts of Satan and
the practices of some sorcerers, the bride was become so dumb,
that she could not so much as open her mouth.

But when this dumb bride saw the Lady Mary entering into
the town, and carrying the Lord Christ in her arms, she stretched
out her hands to the Lord Christ, and took him in her arms,
and closely hugging him, very often kissed him, continually
moving him and pressing him to her body.

Straightway the string of her tongue was loosed, and her
ears were opened, and she began to sing praises unto God,
who had restored her. So there was great joy among the inhabitants of the town that night, who thought that God and
his angels were come down among them.

In this place they abode three days, meeting with the greatest respect and most splendid entertainment. And being then

furnished by the people with provisions for the road, they departed and went to another city, in which they were inclined to lodge, because it was a famous place.

There was in this city a gentlewoman, who, as she went down one day to the river to bathe, behold cursed Satan leaped upon her in the form of a serpent, and folded himself about her belly, and every night lay upon her.

This woman seeing the Lady Mary, and the Lord Christ the infant in her bosom, asked the Lady Mary, that she would give her the child to kiss, and carry in her arms.

When she had consented, and as soon as the woman had moved the child, Satan left her, and fled away, nor did the woman ever afterwards see him. Hereupon all the neighbours praised the Supreme God, and the woman rewarded them with ample beneficence.

On the morrow the same woman brought perfumed water to wash the Lord Jesus; and when she had washed him, she preserved the water. And there was a girl there, whose body was white with a leprosy, who being sprinkled with this water, and washed, was instantly cleansed from her leprosy.

The people therefore said Without doubt Joseph and Mary, and that boy are gods, for they do not look like mortals.

And when they were making ready to go away, the girl, who had been troubled with the leprosy, came and desired they would permit her to go along with them; so they consented and the girl went with them till they came to a city, in which was the palace of a great king, and whose house was not far from the inn. Here they stayed, and when the girl went one day to the prince's wife, and found her in a sorrowful and mournful condition, she asked her the reason of her tears.

She replied, "Wonder not at my groans, for I am under a great misfortune, of which I dare not tell any one."

"But," says the girl, "if you will entrust me with your private grievance, perhaps I may find you a remedy for it."

"Thou, therefore," says the prince's wife, "shalt keep the secret, and not discover it to any one alive! I have been married to this prince, who rules as king over large dominions, and lived long with him, before he had any child by me. At length I conceived by him, but alas! I brought forth a leprous son; which, when he saw, he would not own to be his, but said to me, 'Either do thou kill him, or send him to some nurse in such a place, that he may be never heard of; and now take care of yourself; I will never see you more.'

"So here I pine, lamenting my wretched and miserable circumstances. Alas, my son! alas, my husband! Have I disclosed it to you?"

The girl replied, "I have found a remedy for your disease, which I promise you, for I also was leprous, but God hath cleansed me, even he who is called Jesus, the son of the Lady Mary."

The woman inquiring where that god was, whom she spake of, the girl answered, "He lodges with you here in the same house."

"But how can this be?" says she; "where is he?"

"Behold," replied the girl, "Joseph and Mary; and the infant who is with them is called Jesus: and it is he who delivered me from my disease and torment."

"But by what means," says she, "were you cleansed from your leprosy? Will you not tell me that?"

"Why not?" says the girl; "I took the water with which his body had been washed, and poured it upon me, and my leprosy vanished."

The prince's wife then arose and entertained them, providing a great feast for Joseph among a large company of men. And the next day took perfumed water to wash the Lord Jesus, and afterwards poured the same water upon her son, whom she had brought with her, and her son was instantly cleansed from his leprosy.

Then she sang thanks and praises unto God, and said, "Blessed is the mother that bare thee, O Jesus! Dost thou thus cure men of the same nature with thyself, with the water with which thy body is washed?"

She then offered very large gifts to the Lady Mary, and sent her away with all imaginable respect.

They came afterwards to another city, and had a mind to lodge there. Accordingly they went to a man's house, who was newly married, but by the influence of sorcerers could not enjoy his wife. But they lodging at his house that night, the man was freed of his disorder.

And when they were preparing early in the morning to go forward on their journey, the new married person hindered them, and provided a noble entertainment for them.

But going forward on the morrow, they came to another city, and saw three women going from a certain grave with great weeping.

When Mary saw them, she spake to the girl who was their companion, saying, "Go and inquire of them, what is the matter with them, and what misfortune has befallen them?"

When the girl asked them, they made her no answer, but asked her again, "Who are ye, and where are ye going? For the day is far spent, and the night is at hand."

"We are travellers," saith the girl, "and are seeking for an inn to lodge at."

They replied, "Go along with us, and lodge with us."

They then followed them, and were introduced into a new house, well furnished with all sorts of furniture. It was now winter-time, and the girl went into the parlour where these women were, and found them weeping and lamenting, as before.

By them stood a mule, covered over with silk, and an ebony collar hanging down from his neck, whom they kissed, and were feeding.

But when the girl said, "How handsome, ladies, that mule is!" they replied with tears, and said, "This mule, which you see, was our brother, born of this same mother as we.

"For when our father died, and left us a very large estate, and we had only this brother, and we endeavoured to procure him a suitable match, and thought he should be married as other men, some giddy and jealous woman bewitched him without our knowledge.

"And we, one night, a little before day, while the doors of the house were all fast shut, saw this our brother was changed into a mule, such as you now see him to be. And we, in the melancholy condition in which you see us, having no father to comfort us, have applied to all the wise men, magicians, and diviners in the world, but they have been of no service to us.

"As often therefore as we find ourselves oppressed with grief, we rise and go with this our mother to our father's tomb, where, when we have cried sufficiently we return home."

When the girl had heard this, she said, "Take courage, and cease your fears, for you have a remedy for your afflictions near at hand, even among you and in the midst of your house, for I was also leprous; but when I saw this woman, and this little infant with her, whose name is Jesus, I sprinkled my body with the water with which his mother had washed him, and I was presently made well.

"And I am certain that he is also capable of relieving you under your distress. Wherefore, arise, go to my mistress, Mary, and when you have brought her into your own parlour, disclose to her the secret, at the same time, earnestly beseeching her to be compassionate to you."

As soon as the women had heard the girl's discourse, they hastened away to the Lady Mary, introduced themselves to her, and sitting down before her, they wept, and said, "O our Lady Mary, pity your handmaids, for we have no head of our family, no one older than us; no father, or brother to go in and out before us.

"But this mule, which you see, was our brother, which some woman by witchcraft have brought into this condition which you see: we therefore entreat you to be compassionate to us."

Hereupon Mary was grieved at their case, and taking the Lord Jesus, put him upon the back of the mule, and said to her son, "O Jesus Christ, restore according to thy extraordinary

power this mule, and grant him to have again the shape of a
man and a rational creature, as he had formerly."

This was scarce said by the Lady Mary, but the mule immediately passed into a human form, and became a young man
without any deformity.

Then he and his mother and the sisters worshipped the Lady
Mary, and lifting the child upon their heads, they kissed him,
and said, "Blessed is thy mother, O Jesus, O Saviour of the
world! Blessed are the eyes which are so happy as to see thee."

Then both the sisters told their mother, saying, "Of a truth our
brother is restored to his former shape by the help of the Lord
Jesus Christ, and the kindness of that girl, who told us of Mary
and her son. And inasmuch as our brother is unmarried, it is fit
that we marry him to this girl their servant."

When they had consulted Mary in this matter, and she had
given her consent, they made a splendid wedding for this girl.
And so their sorrow being turned into gladness, and their
mourning into mirth, they began to rejoice, and to make merry,
and sing, being dressed in their richest attire, with bracelets.

Afterwards they glorified and praised God, saying, O Jesus
son of David who changest sorrow into gladness, and mourning
into mirth!

After this Joseph and Mary tarried there ten days, then went
away, having received great respect from those people; who,
when they took their leave of them, and returned home, cried,
but especially the girl. . . .

When they came afterwards into the city Bethlehem, they
found there were several very desperate distempers, which became so troublesome to children by seeing them, that most of
them died. There was there a woman who had a sick son,
whom she brought, when he was at the point of death, to the
Lady Mary, who saw her when she was washing Jesus Christ.

Then said the woman, "O my Lady Mary, look down upon
this my son, who is afflicted with most dreadful pains."

Mary hearing her, said, "Take a little of that water with
which I have washed my son, and sprinkle it upon him."

Then she took a little of that water, as Mary had commanded, and sprinkled it upon her son, who being wearied with his violent pains, had fallen asleep; and after he had slept a little, awaked perfectly well and recovered.

The mother being abundantly glad of this success, went again to Mary, and Mary said to her, "Give praise to God, who hath cured this thy son."

There was in the same place another woman, a neighbour of her, whose son was now cured. This woman's son was afflicted with the same disease, and his eyes were now almost quite shut, and she was lamenting for him day and night.

The mother of the child which was cured, said to her, "Why do you not bring your son to Mary, as I brought my son to her, when he was in the agonies of death; and he was cured by that water, with which the body of her son Jesus was washed?"

When the woman heard her say this, she also went, and having procured the same water, washed her son with it, whereupon his body and his eyes were instantly restored to their former state.

And when she brought her son to Mary, and opened his case to her, she commanded her to give thanks to God for the recovery of her son's health, and tell no one what had happened. . . .

Another woman likewise lived there, whose son was possessed by Satan. This boy, named Judas, as often as Satan seized him, was inclined to bite all that were present; and if he found no one else near him, he would bite his own hands and other parts. But the mother of this miserable boy, hearing of Mary and her son Jesus, arose presently, and taking her son in her arms, brought him to the Lady Mary.

In the meantime, James and Joses had taken away the infant, the Lord Jesus, to play at a proper season with other children; and when they went forth, they sat down and the Lord Jesus with them.

Then Judas, who was possessed, came and sat down at the right hand of Jesus. When Satan was acting upon him as usual, he went about to bite the Lord Jesus. And because he could not do it, he struck Jesus on the right side, so that he cried out. And in the same moment Satan went out of the boy, and ran away like a mad dog.

This same boy who struck Jesus, and out of whom Satan went in the form of a dog, was Judas Iscariot, who betrayed him to the Jews. And that same side, on which Judas struck him, the Jews pierced with a spear. . . .

In the month Adar Jesus gathered together the boys, and ranked them as though he had been a king. For they spread their garments on the ground for him to sit on; and having made a crown of flowers, put it upon his head, and stood on his right and left as the guards of a king.

And if any one happened to pass by, they took him by force, and said, "Come hither, and worship the king, that you may have a prosperous journey."

In the mean time, while these things were doing, there came certain men, carrying a boy upon a couch; for this boy having gone with his companions to the mountain to gather wood, and having found there a partridge's nest, and put his hand in to take out the eggs, was stung by a poisonous serpent, which leaped out of the nest; so that he was forced to cry out for the help of his companions; who, when they came found him lying upon the earth like a dead person. After which his neighbours came and carried him back into the city.

But when they came to the place where the Lord Jesus was sitting like a king, and the other boys stood around him like his ministers, the boys made haste to meet him, who was bitten by the serpent, and said to his neighbours, "Come and pay your respects to the king."

But when, by reason of their sorrow, they refused to come, the boys drew them, and forced them against their wills to come.

And when they came to the Lord Jesus, he inquired, On what account they carried that boy?

And when they answered, that a serpent had bitten him, the Lord Jesus said to the boys, "Let us go and kill that serpent."

But when the parents of the boy desired to be excused, because their son lay at the point of death; the boys made answer, and said, "Did not ye hear what the king said? 'Let us go and kill the serpent'; and will not ye obey him?"

So they brought the couch back again, whether they would or not.

And when they were come to the nest, the Lord Jesus said to the boys, "Is this the serpent's lurking place?" They said, "It is."

Then the Lord Jesus calling the serpent, it presently came forth and submitted to him; to whom he said, "Go and suck out all the poison which thou hast infused into that boy."

So the serpent crept to the boy, and took away all its poison again. Then the Lord Jesus cursed the serpent so that it immediately burst asunder, and died. And he touched the boy with his hand to restore him to his former health.

And when he began to cry, the Lord Jesus said, "Cease crying, for hereafter thou shalt be my disciple."

And this is that Simon the Canaanite, who is mentioned in the Gospel.[13]

THE CHILD JESUS AND JOHN

The following odd bit is a fragment from a manuscript called "The Life of John According to Serapion," a bishop of Thmuis in Egypt during the fourth century. Originally written in Arabic it has been translated by A. Mingana. The "holy John" is identified by the name of his mother, Elizabeth, as the boy who later became known as John the Baptist. The Salome mentioned here is probably the woman believed to have been the sister of Mary.

After five years the pious and blessed old mother Elizabeth passed away, and the holy John sat weeping over her, as he did not know how to shroud her and bury her, because on the day of her death he was only seven years and six months old. . . .

The Lord Jesus Christ who with his eyes sees heaven and earth saw his kinsman John sitting and weeping near his mother, and he also began to weep for a long time, without anyone knowing the cause of his weeping. When the mother of Jesus saw him weeping, she said to him: "Why are you weeping? Did the old man Joseph or any other one chide you?" And the mouth that was full of life answered: "No, O my mother, the real reason is that your kinswoman, the old Elizabeth, has left my beloved John an orphan. He is now weeping over her body which is lying in the mountain."

When the Virgin heard this she began to weep over her kinswoman, and Jesus said to her: "Do not weep, O my virgin mother, you will see her in this very hour." And while he was still speaking with his mother, behold a luminous cloud came down and placed itself between them. And Jesus said: "Call Salome and let us take her with us." And they mounted the cloud which flew with them to the wilderness of 'Ain Kārim and to the spot where lay the body of the blessed Elizabeth, and where the holy John was sitting.

The Saviour said then to the cloud: "Leave us here at this side of the spot." And it immediately went, reached that spot, and departed. Its noise, however, reached the ears of John, who, seized with fear, left the body of his mother. A voice reached him immediately and said to him: "Do not be afraid, O John. I am Jesus Christ, your master. I am your kinsman Jesus, and I came to you with my beloved mother in order to attend to the business of the burial of the blessed Elizabeth, your happy mother, because she is my mother's kinswoman." When the blessed and holy John heard this, he turned back, and Christ the Lord and his virgin mother embraced him. Then the Saviour said to his virgin mother: "Arise, you and Salome, and wash the body." And they washed the body of the blessed Elizabeth in the spring from which she used to draw water for herself and her son. Then the holy Virgin Mary got hold of the blessed (John) and wept over him, and cursed Herod on account of the numerous crimes which he had committed. Then

Michael and Gabriel came down from heaven and dug a grave; and the Saviour said to them: "Go and bring the soul of Zacharias, and the soul of the priest Simeon, in order that they may sing while you bury the body." And Michael brought immediately the souls of Zacharias and Simeon who shrouded the body of Elizabeth and sang for a long time over it. . . .

And Jesus Christ and his mother stayed near the blessed and the holy John seven days, and condoled with him at the death of his mother, and taught him how to live in the desert. And the day of the death of the blessed Elizabeth was the 15th of February.

Then Jesus Christ said to his mother: "Let us now go to the place where I may proceed with my work." The Virgin Mary wept immediately over the loneliness of John, who was very young, and said: "We will take him with us, since he is an orphan without anyone." But Jesus said to her: "This is not the will of my Father who is in the heavens. He shall remain in the wilderness till the day of his showing unto Israel. Instead of a desert full of wild beasts, he will walk in a desert full of angels and prophets, as if they were multitudes of people. Here is also Gabriel, the head of the angels, whom I have appointed to protect him and to grant to him power from heaven. Further, I shall render the water of this spring of water as sweet and delicious to him as the milk he sucked from his mother. Who took care of him in his childhood? Is it not I, O my mother, who love him more than all the world? Zacharias also loved him, and I have ordered him to come and inquire after him, because although his body is buried in the earth, his soul is alive. . . ."

These words the Christ our Lord spoke to his mother, while John was in the desert. And they mounted the cloud, and John looked at them and wept, and Mary wept also bitterly over him, saying: "Woe is me, O John, because you are alone in the desert without anyone. Where is Zacharias, your father, and where is Elizabeth, your mother? Let them come and weep with me today."

And Jesus Christ said to her: "Do not weep over this child, O my mother. I shall not forget him." And while he was uttering these words, behold the clouds lifted them up and brought them to Nazareth. And he fulfilled there everything pertaining to humanity except sin.[14]

THE EDUCATION OF THE CHILD

The familiar gospels of the conventional New Testament are completely silent about the education of Jesus—unless one regards the story of his "sitting in the midst of the doctors, both hearing them and asking them questions," when he was twelve years old and Joseph and Mary took him to Jerusalem at the time of the feast of the Passover, as relating to the youth's education. (Luke 2:40–52.) But there are several versions of the story of Joseph's turning him over to teachers, all of whom found that the lad knew more than they did. Here, as in many other instances, the apocryphal authors seem to have been trying to fill in a gap in the story as it had been told in the conventional Scriptures. The version which follows is from The Gospel of Thomas, regarded by several early church fathers as heretical. It occurs in several languages. The earliest version of it seems to have appeared in the fifth or six century of the Christian era.

There was a man named Zacheus who came to Joseph and said, "Thou hast a wise child; deliver him to me to learn letters, and when he is learned in the study of the letters I will teach him reverently that he become not foolish."

Joseph answered, "No man is able to teach him but God only."

But when Jesus heard Joseph, he said unto Zacheus, "Verily, O master, all things that proceed out of my mouth are true. I am before all men and I am Lord, but ye are the children of strangers. . . ."

But the Jews who stood by and heard the words which Jesus

spake marvelled and said, "Now have we seen such wonders and heard such words from this child as we have never heard neither shall hear from any other man, neither from the chief priests nor the doctors nor the Pharisees."

Jesus answered, "Wherefore marvel ye? Do you think it a thing incredible that I have told you the truth? I know when ye were born and your fathers; and if I say more unto you, I know when the world was created and who sent me unto you."

When the Jews heard the word which the child spake they were wroth, for they were not able to answer him.

And Joseph took the child Jesus to the house where other children were also taught. And he [Jesus] said, "I ought to teach thee and not thou teach me. I know the letters that thou wouldst teach me." And beginning the line he spoke all the letters from A even unto T fully with much quickness.

Now Zacheus cried out, "Woe is me for I am confounded. I have hired shame unto myself by means of this child." And he said unto Joseph, "I beseech thee earnestly, my brother, take him away from me, for I cannot look upon his face nor hear his mighty words. For this child is able to subdue the fire and to restrain the sea, for he was born before the worlds. What womb bare him or what manner of mother brought him up, I know not. O my friends, I am astray in my wits; I am mocked, wretched man that I am. I said I had a disciple, but he is found to be my master. I cannot overcome my shame, for I am old, and I cannot find wherewithal to answer him, so that I am like to fall into heavy sickness and depart out of the world or go away from this city, for all men have seen my shame, that a child hath ensnared me. What can I answer any man or what words can I speak, for he hath overcome me at the first letter! I am confounded, O my friends and acquaintances, and I can find neither first nor last to answer him. And now I beseech thee, brother Joseph, remove him from me, and take him unto thine house, for either he is a sorcerer or a god, or an angel, and what to say I know not."[15]

3

---◆---

THE LOST YEARS

The apocryphal books say little about the years between the childhood of Jesus and his trial and crucifixion, save for a number of sayings, many of which will be included later in this book. There is, however, a strange document which was published in 1894 under the title The Unknown Life of Jesus Christ from Buddhistic Sources, *by one Nicolas Notovich. According to Notovich's account of his discovery of the material, he was traveling in India, where he broke a leg and was taken in and cared for by the monks of a monastery at Leh. There he found, he reported, a record of the stay of "St. Issa," in the monastery (obviously meant to be Jesus of Nazareth), where he learned much from the sacred books of Hinduism and Buddhism, and taught much that was both good Buddhism and good doctrine as the gospels report that of Jesus.*

The book has been declared by scholars to be an obvious hoax —a very successful one, for it sold widely in several languages. A few selections from it, however, are included here, for it is an interesting echo of a widespread legend that Jesus spent in Tibet the unrecorded years between his appearance in the temple at the age of twelve and the beginning of his ministry. As to its obvious lack of historical value, perhaps it is no less reliable than is some of the material in the books that are acknowledged as parts of the Apocryphal New Testament.

In his fourteenth year young Issa, the Blessed One, came this side of the Sindh and settled among the Aryas, in the country

beloved by God. . . . But he left . . . and went to Djagguernat,
in the country of Orsis where repose the mortal remains of
Vyassa-Krishna, and where the white priests of Brahma wel-
comed him joyfully. They taught him to read and to understand
the Vedas, to cure physical ills by means of prayers, to teach
and to expound the sacred scriptures, to drive out evil desires
from man and make him again in the likeness of God.

He spent six years in Djagguernat . . . and in other holy
cities. The common people loved Issa, for he lived in peace
with the Vaisyas and the Sudras, to whom he taught the holy
scriptures. But the Brahmins and the Kshatriyas told him that
they were forbidden by the great Para-Brahma to come near
those who were created from his belly and his feet [that is, the
Vaisya and Sudra castes], that the Vaisyas might only hear the
recital of the Vedas, and this only on the festal days, and that
the Sudras were not only forbidden to attend the reading of the
Vedas, but even to look on them, for they were condemned to
perpetual servitude, as slaves of the Brahmins, and even the
Vaisyas.

"Death alone can enfranchise them from their servitude," has
said Para-Brahma. "Therefore leave them and come to adore
with us the gods, whom you will make angry if you disobey
them."

But Issa, disregarding their words, remained with the Sudras,
preaching against the Brahmins and the Kshatriyas. He de-
claimed strongly against man's arrogating to himself the authority to deprive his fellow-beings of their human and spiritual
rights.

"Verily," he said, "God has made no difference between his
children, who are all alike dear to him."

Issa denied the divine inspiration of the Vedas and the
Puranas, for, as he taught his followers, "One law has been
given to man to guide him in his actions: 'Fear the Lord, thy
God; bend thy knees only before him, and bring to him only
the offerings that come from thy earnings. . . .

"The eternal Judge, the eternal Spirit, constitutes the only and indivisible soul of the universe, and it is this soul alone which creates, contains, and vivifies all. He alone has willed and created. He alone has existed from eternity, and his existence will be without end; there is no one like unto him either in the heavens or on the earth. . . .

"He willed and the world was. By one divine thought he reunited the waters and separated them from the dry land of the globe. He is the cause of the mysterious life of man, into whom he breathed part of his divine being. . . .

"The anger of God will soon break forth upon man, for he has forgotten his creator, and he adores a number of creatures which God has subordinated to him, and to gain favor with images of stone and metal he sacrifices human beings in whom dwells part of the spirit of the Most High. And he humiliates those who work in the sweat of their brows, to gain favor in the eyes of the idler who sitteth at a sumptuous table.

"Those who deprive their brothers of divine happiness will themselves be deprived of it; and the Brahmins and the Kshatriyas shall become the Sudras of the Sudras, with whom the Eternal will stay forever. In the day of judgement the Sudras and the Vaisyas will be forgiven for that they knew not the light, while God will let loose his wrath upon those who arrogated his authority."

The Vaisyas and the Sudras were filled with great admiration, and asked how they should pray, in order not to lose their hold on eternal life.

"Pray not to idols, for they cannot hear you; hearken not to the Vedas where the truth is altered; be humble and humiliate not your fellow-man. Help the poor, support the weak, do evil to none; covet not that which ye have not and which belongs to others."

The white priests and the warriors [that is, the Brahmins and Kshatriyas], who had learned of Issa's discourse to the Sudras, resolved upon his death, and sent their servants to find the young teacher and slay him. But Issa, warned by the Sudras of his danger, left by night . . . and settled in the country of the

Gautamides, where the great Buddha Sakyamundi came to the world, among a people who worshipped the only and sublime Brahma.

When the just Issa had acquired the Pali language, he applied himself to the study of the sacred scrolls of the Sutras. After six years of study Issa, whom the Buddha had elected to spread his holy word, could expound perfectly the sacred scrolls.

He then left . . . and directed his steps toward the west, everywhere preaching to the people the supreme perfection attainable by man, and the good he must do to his fellow-men, which is the sure means of speedy union with the eternal spirit. "He who has recovered his primitive purity," said Issa, "shall die with his transgressions forgiven and have the right to contemplate the majesty of God."*

When the divine Issa traversed the territories of the Pagans he taught that the adoration of visible gods was contrary to natural law.

"For to man," said he, "it has not been given to see the image of God, and it behooves him not to make for himself a multitude of divinities in the imagined likeness of the Eternal. Moreover it is against human conscience to have less regard for the greatness of divine purity than for animals or works of stone or metal made by the hands of man. The Eternal Lawgiver is One; there are no other gods than he; he has parted the world with none, nor had he any counsellor.

"Even as a father shows kindness toward his children, so will God judge men after death, in conformity with his merciful laws. He will never humiliate his child by casting his soul into the body of a beast." . . .

The words of Issa spread among the Pagans through whose country he passed, and the inhabitants abandoned their idols. Seeing this, the priests demanded of him who thus glorified the name of the true God, that he should, in the presence of the

* Cf., "Whosoever shall not receive the kingdom of God as a little child, he shall not enter therein." (Mark 10:15.) —Ed.

people, prove the charges that he made against them, and demonstrate the vanity of their idols.

And Issa answered them: "If your idols, or the animals you worship, really possess the supernatural powers you claim, let them strike me with a thunderbolt before you."

"Why dost not thou perform a miracle," replied the priests, "and let thy God confound ours, if he is greater than they?"

But Issa said, "The miracles of our God have been wrought from the first day when the universe was created; and are performed every day and every moment; whoso sees them not is deprived of one of the most beautiful gifts of life. And it is not on inanimate objects of stone, wood, or metal, that he will let his anger fall, but on the men who worship them, and who, therefore, for their salvation must destroy the idols they have made.

"Even as a stone and a grain of sand, which are naught before man, await patiently their use by him, in like manner, man, who is naught before God, must await in resignation his pleasure for a manifestation of his favor. But woe to you, ye adversaries of men, if it is not the favor you await, but rather the wrath of the Most High; woe to you, if you demand that he attest his power by a miracle!" . . . .

Issa furthermore taught the Pagans that they should not endeavor to see the Eternal Spirit with their eyes; but to perceive him with their hearts, and make themselves worthy of his favors by the purity of their souls.

"Not only," he said to them, "you must refrain from offering human sacrifices, but ye may not lay on the altar any creature to which life has been given, for all things are for man.

"Withhold not from your neighbor his just due, for this would be like stealing from him what he has earned in the sweat of his brow.

"Deceive none, that ye may not yourselves be deceived; seek to justify yourselves before the last judgment, for then it will be too late.

"Be not given to debauchery, for it is a violation of the law of God. That you may attain to supreme bliss ye must not only purify yourselves, but must also guide others into the path that will enable them to regain their primitive innocence."

The countries round about were filled with the renown of Issa's preaching, and when he came to Persia, the priests grew afraid and forbade the people hearing him. Nevertheless the villages received him with joy, and the people harkened intently to his words, which, being seen by the priests, caused them to order that he should be arrested and brought before their high priest, who asked him,

"Of what new god dost thou speak? Knowest thou not, unfortunate man that thou art, the Saint Zoroaster is the only just one, to whom alone was vouchsafed the honor of receiving revelations from the Most High, by whose command the angels compiled his word in laws for the governance of his people, which were given to Zoroaster in Paradise? Who, then, art thou, who darest to utter blasphemies against our God, and sow doubt in the hearts of believers?"

And Issa said, "I preach no new God, but our celestial Father, who has existed before the beginning and will exist until after the end. Of him I have spoken to the people who—even as innocent children—are incapable of comprehending God by their own intelligence or fathoming the sublimity of the divine spirit. But as the new-born child in the night recognizes the mother's breast, so your people, held in the darkness of error by your pernicious doctrines and religious ceremonies, have recognized instinctively their Father, in the Father, whose prophet I am.

"The Eternal Being says to your people by my mouth, 'You shall not adore the sun, for it is but a part of the universe which I have created for man. It rises to warm you during your work, and sets to accord to you the rest that I have ordained. To me only you owe all that you possess, all that surrounds you, and that is above and below you.'"

"But," said the priests, "how could the people live according to your rules if they had no teachers?"

Whereupon Issa answered, "So long as they had no priests,

they were governed by their natural law and conserved the simplicity of their souls. Their souls were in God and to commune with the Father they had not to have recourse to the intermediation of idols, or animals, or fire, as taught by you. You pretend that man must adore the sun, and the Genii of Good and Evil. But I say unto you that your doctrine is pernicious. The sun does not act spontaneously, but by the will of the invisible Creator, who has given it being." . . .

When the Magi heard these words they feared to themselves to do him harm, but at night, when the whole city slept, they brought him outside the walls and left him on the highway in the hope that he would become the prey of wild beasts. But, protected by the Lord our God, Saint Issa continued on his way without accident.[1]

4

THE NATURE AND APPEARANCE OF JESUS

The canonical gospels, Matthew, Mark, Luke, and John, are in agreement at least in their present forms—there is some reason to believe that they may not have been originally—as to the immaculate conception, and the uniquely divine nature of Jesus. The authors of some of the apocryphal books were less sure of this. Also, while there is no physical description of Jesus in the canonical gospels, there is more than one in the Apocrypha, as the following selections show.

And they [the Ebionites] receive the Gospel according to Matthew. . . . And they call it according to the Hebrews, as the truth is that Matthew alone of New Testament writers made this exposition and preaching of the Gospel in Hebrew and in Hebrew letters.

In the Gospel they have it is contained that there was a certain man named Jesus, and he was about thirty years old, who chose us.

John was baptizing, and there went unto him Pharisees and were baptized, and all of Jerusalem. And John had raiment of camel's hair and a leathern girdle about his loins; and his meat (it saith) was wild honey, whereof the taste is the taste of manna, as a cake dipped in oil. . . .

These Ebionites were vegetarians and objected to the idea of eating locusts. . . .

And the beginning of their Gospel says that: It came to pass in the days of Herod, the king of Judaea (when Caiaphas was high priest) that there came a certain man, John by name, baptizing with the baptism of repentance in the river Jordan, who was said to be of the lineage of Aaron, the priest, child of Zacharias and Elizabeth, and all went out to him.

After the people were baptized Jesus also came and was baptized by John; and as he came up from the water, the heavens were opened and he saw the Holy Ghost in the likeness of a dove that descended and entered into him; and a voice from heaven saying, "Thou art my beloved son, in thee I am well pleased," and again, "This day I have begotten thee." And straightway about the place there shone a great light. Which, when John saw it he saith unto him, "Who art thou, Lord?" And again there was a voice from heaven saying unto him, "This is my beloved son in whom I am well pleased."

And then John fell down before him and said, "I beseech thee, Lord, baptize thou me."

But he prevented him, saying, "Suffer it for thus it behoveth that all things should be fulfilled."

And on this account they say that Jesus was begotten of the seed of man, and was chosen, and by the choice of God he was called the Son of God from the Christ that came into him from above in the likeness of a dove. And they deny that he was begotten of God the Father, but say that he was created, as one of the archangels, yet greater, and that he is Lord of angels and of all things made by the Almighty, and that he came and taught, as the Gospel current among them contains, that "I came to destroy the sacrifices, and if ye cease not from sacrificing, the wrath of God will not cease from you."[1]

They of Nazareth thought that Jesus was the son of Joseph and Mary; but the brothers of Jesus, some (founding on a tradition of the Gospel entitled according to Peter, or of the

Book of James) say were sons of Joseph by a former wife who lived with him before Mary.[2]

It is written in the Gospel to the Hebrews that when Christ wished to come upon the earth to men, the Good Father called a mighty power in the heavens and committed Christ to the care thereof. And the power came down into the world and it was called Mary, and Christ was in her womb seven months. Afterwards she gave birth to him, and he increased in stature, and he chose the apostles, was crucified, and taken up by the Father.[3]

[John said] when he had chosen Peter and Andrew, which were brethren, he cometh unto me and James, my brother, saying, "I have need of you, come unto me."

And my brother hearing that said, "John what would this child have that is upon the seashore and called us?"

And I said, "What child?"

And he said to me, "That which beckoneth to us."

And I answered, "Because of our long watch at sea thou seest not aright, my brother James; but seest thou not the man that standeth there, comely and fair and of a cheerful countenance?"

But he said to me, "Him I see not, brother, but let us go forth and see what he would have."

And so when we had brought the ship to land . . . again he was seen of me as having a head rather bald, but the beard thick and flowing, but of James as a youth whose beard was newly come. . . . And after that, as we followed him, both of us were by little and little perplexed as we considered the matter. Yet unto me there yet appeared this yet more wonderful thing: for I would try to see him privily, and I never at any time saw his eyes closing, but only open.* And often he would appear to me as a small man and uncomely, and then again as one reaching unto heaven. And also there was in him

* In Hindu belief this is one of the signs of a god. —Ed.

another marvel: when I sat at meat he would take me upon his own breast; and sometimes his breast was felt to me to be smooth and tender, and sometimes hard like unto stones. . . .

Another glory also will I tell you, brethren: Sometimes when I would lay hold of him I met with a material and solid body, and at other times when I felt him, the substance was immaterial as if it existed not at all.[4]

There hath appeared in these times, and still is, a man of great power named Jesus Christ, who is called by the Gentiles the prophet of truth, who his disciples call the son of God, raising the dead and healing diseases, a man in stature middling tall, and comely, having a reverend countenance, which they that look upon may love and fear; having hair the hue of an unripe hazel-nut and smooth almost down to the ears, but from the ears in curling locks somewhat darker and more shining, waving over his shoulders; having a parting at the middle of the head according to the fashion of the Nazareans; a brow which a moderate color makes beautiful; with a nose and mouth no fault at all can be found; having a full beard of the color of his hair, not long, but a little forked at the chin; having an expression simple and mature, the eyes grey, glancing, and clear; in rebuke terrible, in admonition kind and lovable, cheerful, yet keeping gravity; sometimes he hath wept, but never laughed; in stature of body tall and straight, with hands and arms fair to look upon; in talk grave, reserved and modest, fairer than the children of men.*[5]

At that time there appeared a certain man of magical powers, if it is possible to call him a man, whom certain Greeks call a son of God, but his disciples the true prophet, said to raise the dead and heal all diseases.

His nature and form were human; a man of simple appearance,

---

* Scholars consider that this document can "hardly be earlier than the thirteenth century," and probably inspired by conventional paintings of Jesus.

three cubits high, mature age, dark skin, small stature, hunch-
backed, with a long face, long nose, and meeting eyebrows, so
that those who see him might be affrighted, with scanty hair
with a parting in the middle of his head, after the manner of
the Nazarites, and with an undeveloped beard.[6]

The Avatara is the messenger of God. He is like the viceroy
of a mighty monarch. As when there is some disturbance in a
far-off province the king sends his viceroy to quell it, so when-
ever there is a decline of religion in any part of the world God
sends his Avatara there. It is one and the same Avatara that,
having plunged into the ocean of life, rises up in one place and
is known as Krishna, and diving down again, rises in another
place and is known as Christ. The Avataras, such as Rama,
Krishna, Buddha, Christ, stand in the same relation to the
Absolute Brahman as the waves of the ocean to the ocean.[7]

Verily we gave unto Moses the Scripture, and we caused
a train of messengers to follow after him, and we gave unto
Jesus, son of Mary clear proofs of Allah's sovereignty, and we
supported him with the holy spirit.

Say (O Muslims): We believe in Allah and that which is
revealed unto us and that which was revealed to Abraham, and
Ishmael, and Isaac, and Jacob, and the tribes, and that which
Moses and Jesus received. . . . We make no distinction between
any of them, and unto him have we surrendered.

Of the messengers, some of which we have caused to excel
others, and of whom there are some of them he exalted above
others, and we gave Jesus clear proof. . . .

Some say we slew the Messiah, Jesus, son of Mary, Allah's
messenger. They slew him not nor crucified, but it appeared
so to them; and lo! those who disagree concerning it are in
doubt thereof; they have no knowledge thereof save pursuit of
a conjecture; they slew him not for certain.

O People of the Scripture! Do not exaggerate in your religion
nor utter aught concerning Allah save the truth. The Messiah,

Jesus the son of Mary, was only a messenger of Allah, and his word which he conveyed unto Mary, and a spirit from Him. So believe in Allah and his messengers, and say not "three" . . . Allah is only One God. Far is it removed from his transcendent majesty that he should have a son.[8]

THE SAYINGS OF JESUS

The familiar gospels of the New Testament have specific, often detailed, accounts of the events, the sermons, and parables, of the life of Jesus. The New Testament Apocrypha is almost completely silent concerning the ministry, save for some accounts purporting to have been passed on by the apostles after the death and reported resurrection of Jesus, several groups of sayings, and a short correspondence, almost certainly fictional. The first group of sayings in what follows is from what are called the Oxyrhynchus Papyri, because they are a part of the many fragments of papyri found at Oxyrhynchus, Egypt, from 1897 onwards. They are believed to date in the fourth century A.D., at which time Oxyrhynchus was a center of Christian culture.

Be merciful that ye may obtain mercy; forgive that it may be forgiven unto you; as you do so shall it be done to you; as ye give, so shall it be given unto you; as ye judge, so shall ye be judged; as ye do service, so shall service be done to you; with what measure ye mete, with the same shall it be measured you in return.

He who is near me is near the fire, and he who is far from me is far from the kingdom.

If ye observe not the little, who will give you the great?

They who would see me and reach my kingdom needs must attain me with pain and suffering.

Good must needs come, but blessed is he by whom it cometh; in like manner evil must needs come, but woe unto him by whom it cometh.

The weak shall be saved by the strong.

Be ye mindful of faith and hope, through whom is born that love to God and man which giveth life eternal.

There is a mingling that leadeth to death, and there is a mingling that leadeth to life.

Behold a certain man working on the Sabbath. He said unto him: "Man, if thou knowest what thou doest thou art blest; but if thou knowest not thou art accursed and a transgressor of the law."

Why do ye wonder at signs? I give unto you a mighty inheritance which the whole world doth not contain.

When the Lord was asked by a certain man, when should his kingdom come, he said unto him, "When two shall be one, and the without as the within, and the male with the female, neither male nor female."

Grieve not the Holy Spirit that is in you, and put not out the light which hath shone forth in you.

As ye see yourselves in water or a mirror, so see ye me in yourselves.

Seek for the great and the little shall be added to you; seek for the heavenly and the earthly shall be added to you.

Keep thy flesh pure.

Because of the sick I was sick; because of the hungry I was ahungered; because of the thirsty I was athirst.

Not rendering evil for evil or railing for railing, or fist for fist, or curse for curse.

Love hideth a multitude of sins.

For the Heavenly Father willest the repentance of the sinner rather than his chastisement.

For God willeth that all should receive of his gifts.

Keep that which thou hast and it will be increased into more.

Behold I take the last as the first.

I am come to end the sacrifices, and if ye cease not from sacrificing, the wrath shall not cease from you.

Woe unto him who has made sad the spirit of his brother.

And never rejoice unless ye see your brother also happy.

When Salome asked how long should death hold sway, the

Lord said unto her: So long as ye women bring forth; for I came to end the works of the female. And Salome said unto Him: I have then done well in not bringing forth. And the Lord answered and said: Eat of every pasture, but of that which hath the bitterness [of death] eat not. And when Salome asked when should those things of which she enquired be known, the Lord said: When ye shall tread upon the vesture of shame, and when the two shall be one, and the male with the female neither male nor female.

Pray for your enemies; blessed are they who mourn the destruction of the unbelievers.

I stood on a lofty mountain and saw a gigantic man and another a dwarf and heard as it was a voice of thunder and drew nigh for to hear, and he spake unto me and said, I am thou and thou art I; and wheresoever thou mayest be I am there. In all am I scattered and whencesoever thou willest thou gatherest me, and gathering me thou gatherest thyself.

May thy Holy Spirit come upon us and purify us!

Possess nothing upon the earth.

Though ye be gathered together with me in my bosom, if ye do not my commandments, I will cast you forth.

Gain for yourselves, ye sons of Adam, by means of these transitory things which are not yours, that which is your own, and passeth not away.

For even among the prophets after they have been anointed by the Holy Spirit, the word of sin has been found.

If a man shall abandon all for my name's sake at the second coming he shall inherit eternal life.

If ye make not the below into the above and the above into the below, the right into the left and the left into the right, the before into the behind and the behind into the before, ye shall not enter into the kingdom of God.

I recognized myself, and gathered myself together from all sides; I sowed no children for the ruler, but I tore up his roots, and gathered together [my] limbs that were scattered abroad; I know thee who thou art, for I am from the realms above.

What ye preach with words before the people, do ye in deeds before every man.

Thou art the key [who openest] for every man and shuttest for every man.

Jesus saith: Except ye fast to the world, ye shall in no wise find the Kingdom of God; and except ye sabbatize the Sabbath, ye shall not see the Father.

Jesus saith: I stood in the midst of the world, and in flesh was I seen of them, and I found all drunken, and none found I athirst among them. And my soul grieveth over the souls of men, because they are blind in their heart and see not. . . .

Jesus saith: Wheresoever there be two, they are not without God; and wherever there is one alone, I say, I am with him. Raise the stone, and there thou shalt find me; cleave the wood, and there am I.

Jesus saith: A prophet is not acceptable in his own country, neither doth a physician work cures upon those that know him.

Jesus saith: A city built on the top of a high hill and stablished can neither fall nor be hid.

Jesus saith: Thou hearest with one ear (but the other thou hast closed).

These are the . . . words which Jesus the Living [One] spake to . . . and Thomas, and He said unto [them]: Every one who hearkeneth to these words shall never taste of death.

Jesus saith: Let not him who seeketh . . . cease until he findeth, and when he findeth he shall wonder; wondering he shall reign, and reigning shall rest.

Jesus saith: [Ye ask(?) Who are these] that draw us [to the kingdom if] the kingdom is in Heaven? . . . the fowls of the air, and all beasts that are under the earth or upon the earth, and the fishes of the sea [these are they that draw] you; and the Kingdom of Heaven is within you; and whosoever shall know himself shall find it. [Strive therefore(?)] to know yourselves, and ye shall be aware that ye are the sons of the . . . Father; [and(?)] ye shall know that ye are in [the City of God(?)] and ye are [the City(?)].

Jesus saith: Everything that is not before thy face and that which is hidden from thee shall be revealed to thee. For there is nothing hidden which shall not be made manifest, nor buried which shall not be raised.[9]

In 1945, in the village of Nag Hammadi, Egypt, near the ancient Chenoboskion, some thirteen volumes of Gnostic papyri were discovered. Among them was a work called The Gospel of Thomas, consisting of sayings—some of which had already been discovered in the Oxyrhynchus fragments, from which a number have been cited above. A generous selection from The Gospel of Thomas follows. After its first inclusion, the reiterant statement, "Jesus said," has been omitted.

These are the secret words which Jesus, the living, spoke and which Didymus Judas Thomas wrote. And he said, "He who will find the interpretation of these words will not taste death."

The old man in his days will not hesitate to ask an infant of seven days about the place of life, and he will live. For many of the first will be last, and they will become a single one.

Know what is before your face, and what is hidden from you will be revealed to you; for there is nothing hidden that will not be manifest.

His disciples asked him, "Do you want us to fast? And in what way shall we pray and give alms? And what observances shall we keep in eating?"

Jesus said, "Do not speak falsely, and what you hate, do not do. For all things are revealed before heaven. And there is nothing hidden that will not be manifest, and there is nothing covered that will remain without being uncovered."

Blessed is the lion which man will eat, that the lion may become a man; And cursed is the man whom the lion will eat, that the lion will become a man.

Man is like a wise fisherman, who cast his net in the sea and drew it out of the sea when it was full of little fishes. Among them the wise fisherman found a large good fish. He cast all the little fishes down into the sea. He selected the large fish without difficulty. He who has ears, let him hear.

Behold the sower went forth. He filled his hand; he threw. Some fell on the road. The birds came and gathered them. Others fell upon the rock and sent no root down into the earth and put forth no ear to heaven. And others fell upon thorns. They choked the seed and the worm ate them. And others fell upon the good earth and brought forth fruits up to heaven. At times it came as sixty, and at times as one hundred and twenty.

I have cast a fire upon the world, and lo, I keep it until it burns up.

This heaven will pass away, and the one that is above it will pass away; and that which is dead does not live, and that which lives will not die.

On the days when you were eating that which is dead, you were making it as that which lives. When you come into the light, what will you do?

Today you are as one; you have worked together. But when you become two, what will you do?

Jesus said to his disciples, "Make comparisons; tell me what I am like."

Simon Peter said to him, "You are like a just angel."

Matthew said to him, "You are like a wise philosopher."

Thomas said to him, "Master, my mouth will in no way endure my saying what you are like."

Jesus said, "I am not your master since you drank and became drunk from the bubbling spring which I have distributed."

And he took him, went aside, and said three words. But when Thomas came to his companions, they asked him, "What did Jesus say?" Thomas said to them, "If I tell you one of the words he said to me, you will bring stones and you will cast them at me, and a fire will go forth from the stones and destroy you."

If you fast you will beget for yourselves a sin, and if you pray, you will be condemned, and if you give alms you will do harm to your spirits. And if you go into every land, and travel in the regions, if they receive you, eat what they set before you. Heal the sick among them. That which goeth into your mouth will not defile you; but that which goes out of your mouth, that will defile you.

When you see the one who was not born of woman, cast yourselves down on your faces; he is your father.

Perhaps men think that I came to cast peace on the world; and they do not know that I came to cast division upon the earth, fire, sword, war. For five will be in a house; there will be three against two, and two against three, the father against the son, and the son against the father. And they will stand because they are single ones.

I will give you what eye has not seen and ear has not heard and hand has not touched and which has not come into the heart of man.

The disciples said to Jesus, "Tell us in what way our end will take place."

Jesus said, "You have indeed uncovered the beginning so that you may seek the end; for in the place where the beginning is there the end will be. Blessed is he who will stand in the beginning and will know the end and will not taste death."

Blessed is he who was before he became. If you are my disciples and hear my words these stones will serve you. For you have five trees in Paradise; they do not stir, summer or winter, and their leaves do not fall off. He who will understand them will not taste death.

The disciples said to Jesus, "Tell us what the kingdom of heaven is like."

He said to them, "It is like a grain of mustard, smaller than all the seeds, but when it falls on the earth which is tilled, it sends forth a great branch and becomes covering for the birds of heaven."

Mariham [an early name for Mary, the mother of Jesus] said to Jesus, "What are your disciples like?"

He said, "They are like little children who dwell in a field which is not theirs. When the masters of the field come, they will say, 'Leave our field to us!' They are naked before their eyes, as they leave it to them and give them their field."

If the householder knows that the thief is coming, he will watch before he comes and will not let him dig into his house of his kingdom to carry off his vessels. But you, be watchful over against the world. Gird your loins with a great power so that no robber may find a way to come to you. For the fulfillment of your need which you await will be found. May there be an understanding man in your midst! After the fruit ripened, he came with his sickle in his hand and reaped. He who has ears to hear, let him hear!

Jesus saw little ones receiving milk. He said to his desciples, "These little ones receiving milk are like those who enter the kingdom."

They said to him, "If we are little ones will we enter the kingdom?"

Jesus said to them, "When you make the two one, and the inside like the outside, and the outside like the inside, and the upper side like the under side, and make the man with the woman a single one, in order that the man is not man and the woman not woman; when you make eyes in place of an eye, and a hand in place of a hand, and a foot in place of a foot, and an image in place of an image; then you will go into the kingdom."

I will choose you, one from a thousand and two from ten thousand, and they will stand because they are a single one.

His disciples said, "Show us the place where you are, for it is necessary for us to seek it."

He said to them, "He who has ears to hear, let him hear! There is light within a light man and it illuminates the whole world; if it does not illuminate it it is darkness."

Love your brother as your soul; keep him like the apple of your eye.

You see the splinter in your brother's eye, but you do not see the beam in your own eye. When you cast out the beam from your own eye, then you will see to cast out the splinter from your brother's eye.

If you do not fast to the world, you will not find the kingdom; if you do not truly keep the Sabbath, you will not see the Father.

I stood in the midst of the world and I appeared to them in the flesh; I found all of them drunken; I found none among them thirsty. And my soul was pained for the children of men, for they are blind in their hearts, and they do not see that they came empty into the world seeking also to leave the world empty. But now they are drunken. When they throw off their wine they will repent.

If the flesh came into the world for the sake of the spirit, it is a wonder; but if the spirit came into the world for the sake of the body, it is a wonder of wonders; but I wonder how this great wealth has dwelt in this poverty.

Where there are three gods, they are gods. Where there are two or one, I am with him.

No prophet is acceptable in his village; no physician heals those who know him.

A city built on a high mountain and fortified cannot fall and cannot remain hidden.

What you hear in your ear preach to another upon your roofs. For no one lights a lamp and puts it under a bushel and no one puts it in a hidden place; but he puts it on the lamp stand, so that all who go in and come out may see its light.

If a blind man leads a blind man, both fall into a pit.

It is impossible for anyone to go into the house of a strong man and take it by force unless he binds his hands; then he will plunder the house.

Do not take care from morning to evening and from evening to morning what you will put on yourselves.

His disciples asked, "On what day will you appear to us, and on what day will we see you?"

Jesus said, "When you undress yourselves and are not ashamed, and take your clothing and lay it under your feet like little children and tread on it, then will you become sons of the Living One and you will have no fear."

Many times you have desired to hear these words which I speak to you, and you have no one else from whom to hear them. The days will come when you will seek me and you will not find me.

The Pharisees and scribes received the keys of knowledge; they hid them and did not enter in. But you be wise as serpents and sincere as doves.

A vine was planted outside of the Father, and it has not become strong; it will be uprooted and it will perish.

He who has something in his hand, to him it will be given; and he who has nothing, from him even what he has will be taken away.

Come into being as you pass away.

His disciples said to him, "Who are you that you say these things to us?"

Jesus said, "In what I say to you you do not understand who I am. But you have become like the Jews; for they love the tree and hate its fruit, and they love the fruit and hate the tree."

He who blasphemes the Father will be forgiven, and he who blasphemes the Son will be forgiven, but he who blasphemes the Holy Spirit will not be forgiven on earth or in heaven.

Grapes are not gathered from thorns, nor are figs picked from camel's thorn. They give no fruit. And a good man brings forth good from his treasure. A wicked man brings forth evil from his evil treasure which is in his heart, and says evil things; for from the abundance of his heart he brings forth evil things.

From Adam to John the Baptist no one is greater than John the Baptist, but he among you who will become a little one will understand the kingdom, and will be greater than John.

It is impossible for a man to mount two horses and stretch two bows, and it is impossible for a slave to serve two masters. Either he will honor the one and despise the other, or he will hate the one and love the other. No one drinks old wine and immediately desires to drink new wine. And new wine is not put in old skins, lest they split. And old wine is not put into new skins lest it perish. And an old patch is not put on a new garment since a rip will result.

If two make peace with each other in the same house, they will say to the mountain, Move! and it will move.

If they say to you "Whence have you come?" say to them "We came from the light, the place where the light came into existence through itself alone." If they say to you "Who are you?" say, "We are his sons, and the elect of the living Father." If they ask you "What is the sign of your Father who is within you?" say to them, "It is a movement and a rest."

His disciples said to him, "On what day will the rest of the dead take place? And on what day does the new world come?" He said to them, "That for which you are waiting has come, and you do not recognize it."

His disciples said to him, "Twenty-four prophets spoke in Israel, and all of them spoke concerning you." He said to them, "You have abandoned the one who lives before your eyes, and you have spoken concerning the dead."

His disciples said to him, "Is circumcision profitable or not?" He said to them, "If it were profitable their father would have begotten them circumcised from their mother. But the true circumcision in the spirit has found complete usefulness."

Blessed are the poor, for yours is the kingdom of heaven.

He who will not hate his father and his mother cannot be my disciple. And he who will not hate his brothers and his sisters, and carry the cross as I have, will not become worthy of me.

He who has known the world has found a corpse, and he who has found a corpse of him the world is not worthy.

The kingdom of heaven is like a man who had good seed. His enemies came in the night and sowed tares upon the good seed. The man did not allow the tares to be pulled up. He said to them, "Lest you go that we may pull up the tares, and you pull up the wheat along with it. For on the day of the harvest the tares will appear; they will be pulled up and burned."

Blessed is the man who has labored and found life.

Two will be resting on one bed; the one will die, the other will live.

Salome said, "Who are you, O man? Have you, as from the One mounted my bed and eaten from my table?"

Jesus said to her, "I am he who came into existence from that which is equal; I was given the things of my Father."

Salome said, "I am your disciple."

Jesus said, "Therefore I say, when it is deserted it will be full of light, but when it is shared it will be full of darkness."

There was a rich man who had many possessions. He said, "I will use my possessions so that I may sow and reap and plant and fill my storehouse with fruit, so that I will have no need of anything." Such were the thoughts in his heart. And in that very night he died. He who has ears, let him hear.

Blessed are they who are persecuted in their hearts; they are the ones who have known the Father in truth. Blessed are those who are hungry that the body of him who desires may be satisfied.

If you beget in yourselves him whom you have, he will save you. If you do not have him within yourselves, he whom you do not have within yourselves will kill you.

The harvest is great, but the laborers are few. Pray then the Lord that he may cast laborers into the harvest.

Many stand before the door, but the single ones are those who will enter into the bridechamber.

The kingdom of the Father is like a merchant who had a cargo, and who found a pearl. He was a wise man. Therefore he sold his cargo and bought for himself the pearl alone. You too seek for treasure which does not perish, which abides where no moth enters and worms do not destroy.

I am the light which is over everything. I am the All; the All has gone forth and has returned.

May he who has become rich become a king, and he who has the power deny the world.

Why do you wash the outside of the cup? Do you not know that he who made the inside is also he who made the outside?

They said to him: "Tell us who you are."

He said to them: "You test the face of the heaven and the earth, and you do not know what is before you."

Seek and you will find. . . . Do not give that which is holy to the dogs, lest they cast it on the dung.

The kingdom of the Father is like a woman. She took a little leaven, put it in dough, and made it into large loaves. He who has ears let him hear.

The kingdom is like a woman who carried a vessel full of meal and went a long way. The handle of the vessel broke; the meal flowed out behind her on the way. She did not notice it. . . . When she reached her house she set the vessel down and found it empty.

The kingdom is like a shepherd who had a hundred sheep. One of them, the largest, lost his way. He left the ninety and nine and sought the one until he found it. After he had toiled, he said to the sheep, I love you more than the ninety-nine.

The disciples said to him, "Your brothers and your mother are standing outside." He said to them, "Those who do the will of my Father are my brothers and my mother; they are the ones who will enter into the kingdom of my Father."

He who will not hate his father and his mother as I do, cannot be my disciple. And he who will not love his father and his mother as I do, cannot be my disciple.

Woe to the Pharisees! For they are like a dog which sleeps in the crib of the oxen; for he neither eats nor lets the oxen eat.

Blessed is the man who knows that fierce robbers are entering, so that he arises and is prepared in his strength and girds his loins before they enter.

They said to him, "Come let us pray today and fast." Jesus said, "What sin, then, have I committed or in what have I been overcome? But when the bridegroom comes out of the bride-chamber, then may they fast and pray."

When you make the two one you will become the sons of man, and if you say, "Mountain be removed!" it will move.

Let him who has found the world and become rich deny the world.

He who will find himself, of him the world is not worthy.

Woe to the flesh which hangs upon the soul! Woe to the soul that hangs upon the flesh!

His disciples said to him, "On what day does the kingdom come?" Jesus said, "It does not come when it is expected. They will not say 'Lo here,' or 'Lo there,' but the kingdom of the Father is spread out upon the earth and men do not see it."[10]

There are, however, fragments of another gospel that were found among the Oxyrhynchus Papyri, which relate a supposed episode in the life of Jesus, apparently during his ministry, as well as some of his sayings.

He took them with him and led them to the cleansing place and walked in the temple. And there came near a Pharisee, an high priest, Levi by name, and met them and said to the Savior: "Who hath given thee leave to tread this holy place and to look upon these holy vessels, without first bathing thyself, and without thy disciples having washed their feet, but unclean as thou art hast thou walked in this temple which is a clean place wherein no man walketh but one that hath bathed himself and changed his clothes, nor presumeth to look upon these holy vessels?"

And straightway the Savior stood with his disciples and answered him: "Art thou then clean that art in the temple?"

He said: "I am clean for I have bathed in the pool of David, and when I had gone down into it by the one ladder I came up by the other; and I have put on white and clean raiment, and then did I come, and have looked upon these holy vessels."

The Savior answered him: "Woe unto you, ye blind that see not! Thou hast bathed thyself in these waters that are poured forth, into which, night and day, dogs and swine are cast. And after thou hadst washed thyself didst scour thine outer skin, which the harlots also and flute-girls anoint and bathe and scour and beautify to arouse desire in men, but within it is filled with scorpions and all evil. But I and my disciples, of whom thou sayest that we are not washed, have been washed in living waters which came down from God out of heaven."

A single leaf from the remains of an ancient manuscript of The Acts of Paul contains a longer saying of Jesus.

He said unto them:

"Why marvel ye that I raise the dead, or that I make the lame to go, or that I cleanse the lepers or raise the sick, or that I have healed the palsied and possessed, or that I have parted a few loaves and satisfied many, or that I have walked on the sea or that I have commanded the winds? If ye believe this and are convinced, then are ye great. For verily I say unto you, If ye say unto this mountain, 'Lift thyself and be cast into the sea,' without having doubted in your soul, it shall happen unto you."

One of them whose name was Simon, was convinced, and said:

"O Lord, verily great are the works which thou doest. For we have never heard, nor have we seen ever a man that hath raised the dead save thee."

The Lord said unto him:

"Ye shall pray for the works which I myself shall do, but the other works will I do straightway. For these I do for a momentary salvation in time, in those places where they are, that they may believe on him who sent me."

Simon said unto him:

"O Lord, command me, that I may speak."

He said unto him:

"Speak, Peter," for from that day he did call them by name. He said:

"What then is this work that is greater than these, except the raising of the dead, and the feeding of such a multitude?" The Lord said unto him, "There is somewhat that is greater than this, and blessed are they that have believed with their whole heart."[11]

The following, taken from Against All Heresies *by Irenaeus, a second-century bishop of Lyons, may be the source of the doctrine of the contempory sect called Jehovah's Witnesses, who proclaim that the natural wonders described here will herald the fact that the number of "the elect of Jehovah" has been completed, and that the millennium has come.*

As the elders remember which saw John, the Lord's disciple, that they heard from him how the Lord taught concerning those times, and said, "The days shall come when vines shall grow each having ten thousand branches, and on one branch ten thousand shoots, and on every shoot ten thousand clusters, and in every cluster ten thousand grapes, and every grape, when it is pressed, will yield five and twenty measures of wine. And when any of the saints taketh hold of one of the clusters another will cry out, 'I am a better cluster, take me, through me bless thou the Lord.'"

Likewise he said that a grain of wheat shall bring forth ten thousand ears, and every ear shall have ten thousand grains, and every grain shall yield five double pounds of white, clean, flour; and all other seeds and plants according to the agreement that followeth with them, and all animals using these foods which are got from the earth shall be peaceable and in concord one with another, subject unto men with all obedience.[12]

JESUS AND ABGARUS

The following two letters, undoubtedly fictional, have been discovered in many forms. The versions given are from the Ecclesiastical History *of* Eusebius.

A copy of a letter written by Abgarus the toparch* to Jesus, and sent to him by means of Ananias the runner, to Jerusalem.

Abgarus Uchama the toparch to Jesus the good Saviour that hath appeared in the parts of Jerusalem, greeting. I have heard concerning thee and thy cures, that they are done of thee without drugs or herbs: for, as the report goes, thou makest blind men to see again, lame to walk, and cleansest lepers, and castest out unclean spirits and devils, and those that are afflicted with long sickness thou healest, and raisest the dead. And having heard all this of thee, I had determined one of two things, either that thou art God come down from heaven, and so doest these things, or art a Son of God that doest these things. Therefore now have I written and entreated thee to trouble thyself to come to me and heal the affliction which I have. For indeed I have heard that the Jews even murmur against thee and wish to do thee hurt. And I have a very little city but comely, which is sufficient for us both.

The answer, written by Jesus, sent by Ananias the runner to Abgarus the toparch.

Blessed art thou that hast believed in me, not having seen me. For it is written concerning me that they that have seen me shall not believe in me, and that they that have not seen me shall believe and live. But concerning that which thou hast written to me, to come unto thee; it must needs be that I fulfil all things for the which I was sent here, and after fulfilling them should then be taken up unto him that sent me. And when I am taken up, I will send thee one of my disciples, to heal thine affliction and give life to thee and them that are with thee.[13]

* India was at one time divided into ten toparchies, each ruled by a toparch.

5

---◆---

JESUS CRUCIFIED

PRELUDE TO SUFFERING

*The following brief fragment is part of a papyrus of the fourth,
fifth, or sixth century and is thought to be part of an apocryphal
gospel, but all attempts to identify the gospel have failed. The
text was, when found, severely damaged, and many words and
phrases have been supplied on a conjectural basis by scholars.
The papyrus came into the possession of Strasbourg University
in 1899.*

Now . . . he turned himself to us and said: "The hour is come
when I shall be taken from you. The spirit is willing, but the
flesh is weak: stay and watch with me."

But we the apostles wept . . .

He . . . said unto us: "Fear not because of the destruction of
the body but fear much more . . . the power of darkness. Remember all that I have said unto you: If they have persecuted
me, they will persecute you also. . . . Ye rejoice because I have
overcome the world."[1]

*The Acts of John, from which the following account is taken,
is probably a product of the middle of the second century. It
seems to have been, in its original form, about the same length
as the Gospel according to Matthew, though some of it has now
been lost, including the beginning of the book. It is available*

in a Latin and Greek version, the Latin considerably mutilated.
The part here used is from the Latin version.

Now before he was taken by the lawless Jews, who also were governed by the lawless serpent, he gathered all of us together and said:

"Before I am delivered up unto them let us sing an hymn to the Father, and so go forth to that which lieth before us."

He bade us therefore make as it were a ring, holding one another's hands, and himself standing in the midst he said:

"Answer Amen unto me."

He began, then, to sing an hymn and to say:

"Glory be to thee, Father."

And we, going about in a ring, answered him: "Amen."

"Glory be to thee, Word: Glory be to thee, Grace."

"Amen."

"Glory be to thee, Spirit: Glory be to thee, Holy One: Glory be to thy glory."

"Amen."

"We praise thee, O Father; we give thanks to thee, O Light, wherein darkness dwelleth not."

"Amen."

"Now whereas [*or* wherefore] we give thanks, I say: I would be saved, and I would save."

"Amen."

"I would be loosed, and I would loose."

"Amen."

"I would be wounded, and I would wound."

"Amen."

"I would be born, and I would bear."

"Amen."

"I would eat, and I would be eaten."

"Amen."

"I would hear, and I would be heard."

"Amen."

"I would be thought, being wholly thought."

"Amen."

"I would be washed, and I would wash."

"Amen."

"Grace danceth. I would pipe; dance ye all."

"Amen."

"I would mourn: lament ye all."

"Amen."

"The number Eight singeth praise with us."

"Amen."

"The number Twelve danceth on high."

"Amen."

"The Whole on high hath part in *our* dancing."

"Amen."

"Whoso danceth not, knoweth not what cometh to pass."

"Amen."

"I would flee, and I would stay."

"Amen."

"I would adorn, and I would be adorned."

"Amen."

"I would be united, and I would unite."

"Amen."

"A house I have not, and I have houses."

"Amen."

"A place I have not, and I have places."

"Amen."

"A temple I have not, and I have temples."

"Amen."

"A lamp am I to thee that beholdest me."

"Amen."

"A mirror am I to thee that perceivest me."

"Amen."

"A door am I to thee that knockest at me."

"Amen."

"A way am I to thee a wayfarer."

"Amen."

"Now answer thou unto my dancing. Behold thyself in me

who speak, and seeing what I do, keep silence about my mysteries.

"Thou that dancest, perceive what I do, for thine is this passion of the manhood, which I am about to suffer. For thou couldest not at all have understood what thou sufferest if I had not been sent unto thee, as the word of the Father. Thou that sawest what I suffer sawest me as suffering, and seeing it thou didst not abide but wert wholly moved to make wise. Thou hast me as a bed, rest upon me. Who I am, thou shalt know when I depart. What now I am seen to be, that I am not. Thou shalt see when thou comest. If thou hadst known how to suffer, thou wouldst have been able not to suffer. Learn thou to suffer, and thou shalt be able not to suffer. What thou knowest not, I myself will teach thee. Thy God am I, not the God of the traitor. I would keep tune with holy souls. In me know thou the word of wisdom. Again with me say thou: 'Glory be to thee, Father; glory to thee, Word; glory to thee, Holy Ghost.' And if thou wouldst know concerning me, what I was, know that with a word did I deceive all things and I was no whit deceived. I have leaped: but do thou understand the whole, and having understood it, say: 'Glory be to thee, Father. Amen.'"

Thus, my beloved, having danced with us the Lord went forth.[2]

". . . SUFFERED UNDER PONTIUS PILATE . . ."

The Gospel of Nicodemus, or Acts of Pilate, from which the account of the trial of Jesus has been taken, exists in Latin, Coptic, Greek, Syriac, and Armenian versions, and is probably of the fourth century, though some scholars believe that parts of it are earlier than this. In general it conforms to the account in the familiar gospels of the New Testament, though there are details in it which do not occur in them.

These be the things which, after the cross and passion of the Lord, Nicodemus recorded and delivered unto the high priest and the rest of the Jews: and the same Nicodemus set them forth in Hebrew.

For the chief priests and scribes assembled in council, even Annas and Caiaphas and Somne [Senes] and Dothaim [Dothael, Dathaës, Datam] and Gamaliel, Judas, Levi and Nepthalim, Alexander and Jairus and the rest of the Jews, and came unto Pilate accusing Jesus for many deeds, saying: "We know this man, that he is the son of Joseph the carpenter, begotten of Mary, and he saith that he is the Son of God and a king; moreover he doth pollute the sabbaths and he would destroy the law of our fathers."

Pilate saith: "And what things are they that he doeth, and would destroy the law?"

The Jews say: "We have a law that we should not heal any man on the sabbath: but this man of his evil deeds hath healed the lame and the bent, the withered and the blind and the paralytic, the dumb and them that were possessed, on the sabbath day!"

Pilate saith unto them: "By what evil deeds?"

They say unto him: "He is a sorcerer, and by Beelzebub the prince of the devils he casteth out devils, and they are all subject unto him."

Pilate saith unto them: "This is not to cast out devils by an unclean spirit, but by the god Asclepius."

The Jews say unto Pilate: "We beseech thy majesty that he appear before thy judgement-seat and be heard."

And Pilate called them unto him and said: "Tell me, how can I that am a governor examine a king?"

They say unto him: "We say not that he is a king, but he saith it of himself."

And Pilate called the messenger and said unto him: "Let Jesus be brought hither, but with gentleness."

And the messenger went forth, and when he perceived Jesus he worshipped him and took the kerchief that was on his hand and spread it upon the earth and saith unto him: "Lord, walk hereon and enter in, for the governor calleth thee."

And when the Jews saw what the messenger had done, they cried out against Pilate saying: "Wherefore didst thou not summon him by an herald to enter in, but by a messenger? for the messenger when he saw him worshipped him and spread out his kerchief upon the ground and hath made him walk upon it like a king!"

Then Pilate called for the messenger and said unto him: "Wherefore hast thou done this, and hast spread thy kerchief upon the ground and made Jesus to walk upon it?"

The messenger saith unto him: "Lord governor, when thou sentest me to Jerusalem unto Alexander, I saw Jesus sitting upon an ass, and the children of the Hebrews held branches in their hands and cried out, and others spread their garments beneath him, saying: 'Save now, thou that art in the highest: blessed is he that cometh in the name of the Lord.'"

The Jews cried out and said unto the messenger: "The children of the Hebrews cried out in Hebrew: how then hast thou it in the Greek?"

The messenger saith to them: "I did ask one of the Jews . . . and he interpreted it unto me."

Pilate saith unto them: "And how cried they in Hebrew?"

The Jews say unto him: "'Hosanna membrome barouchamma adonai.'"

Pilate saith unto them: "And the *Hosanna* and the rest, how is it interpreted?"

The Jews say unto him: "Save now, thou that art in the highest: blessed is he that cometh in the name of the Lord."

Pilate saith unto them: "If you yourselves bear witness of the words which were said of the children, wherein hath the messenger sinned?" and they held their peace.

The governor saith unto the messenger: "Go forth and bring him in after what manner thou wilt."

And the messenger went forth and did after the former manner and said unto Jesus: "Lord, enter in: the governor calleth thee."

Now when Jesus entered in, and the ensigns were holding

the standards, the images of the standards bowed and did reverence to Jesus. And when the Jews saw the carriage of the standards, how they bowed themselves and did reverence unto Jesus, they cried out above measure against the ensigns.

But Pilate said unto the Jews: "Marvel ye not that the images bowed themselves and did reverence unto Jesus?"

The Jews say unto Pilate: "We saw how the ensigns made them to bow and did reverence to him."

And the governor called for the ensigns and saith unto them: "Wherefore did ye so?"

They say unto Pilate: "We are Greeks and servers of temples, and how could we do him reverence? for indeed, whilst we held the images they bowed of themselves and did reverence unto him."

Then saith Pilate unto the rulers of the synagogue and the elders of the people: "Choose you out able and strong men and let them hold the standards, and let us see if they bow of themselves."

And the elders of the Jews took twelve men strong and able and made them to hold the standards by sixes, and they were set before the judgement-seat of the governor; and Pilate said to the messenger: "Take him out of the judgement hall and bring him in again after what manner thou wilt."

And Jesus went out of the judgement hall, he and the messenger. And Pilate called unto him them that before held the images, and said unto them: "I have sworn by the safety of Caesar that if the standards bow not when Jesus entereth in, I will cut off your heads."

And the governor commanded Jesus to enter in the second time. And the messenger did after the former manner and besought Jesus much that he would walk upon his kerchief; and he walked upon it and entered in. And when he had entered, the standards bowed themselves again and did reverence unto Jesus.

Now when Pilate saw it he was afraid, and sought to rise up from the judgement-seat. And while he yet thought to rise up, his wife sent unto him, saying: "Have thou nothing to do with this just man, for I have suffered many things because of him by night."

And Pilate called unto him all the Jews, and said unto them: "Ye know that my wife feareth God and favoureth rather the customs of the Jews, with you?"

They say unto him: "Yea, we know it."

Pilate saith unto them: "Lo, my wife hath sent unto me, saying: 'Have thou nothing to do with this just man: for I have suffered many things because of him by night.'"

But the Jews answered and said unto Pilate: "Said we not unto thee that he is a sorcerer? behold, he hath sent a vision of a dream unto thy wife."

And Pilate called Jesus unto him and said to him: "What is it that these witness against thee? speakest thou nothing?"

But Jesus said: "If they had not had power they would have spoken nothing; for every man hath power over his own mouth, to speak good or evil: they shall see to it."

The elders of the Jews answered and said unto Jesus: "What shall we see? Firstly, that thou wast born of fornication; secondly, that thy birth in Bethlehem was the cause of the slaying of children; thirdly, that thy father Joseph and thy mother Mary fled into Egypt because they had no confidence before the people."

Then said certain of them that stood by, devout men of the Jews: "We say not that he came of fornication; but we know that Joseph was betrothed unto Mary, and he was not born of fornication."

Pilate saith unto those Jews which said that he came of fornication: "This your saying is not true, for there were espousals, as these also say which are of your nation."

Annas and Caiaphas say unto Pilate: "The whole multitude of us cry out that he was born of fornication, and we are not believed: but these proselytes and disciples of his."

And Pilate called Annas and Caiaphas unto him and said to them: "What be proselytes?"

They say unto him: "They were born children of Greeks, and now are they become Jews."

Then said they which said that he was not born of fornication, even Lazarus, Asterius, Antonius, Jacob, Amnes, Zenas, Samuel, Isaac, Phinees, Crispus, Agrippa, and Judas: "We were not born proselytes but we are children of Jews and we speak the truth; for verily we were present at the espousals of Joseph and Mary."

And Pilate called unto him those twelve men which said that he was not born of fornication, and saith unto them: "I adjure you by the safety of Caesar, are these things true which ye have said that he was not born of fornication?"

They say unto Pilate: "We have a law that we swear not, because it is sin: but let them swear by the safety of Caesar that it is not as we have said, and we will be guilty of death."

Pilate saith to Annas and Caiaphas: "Answer ye nothing to these things?"

Annas and Caiaphas say unto Pilate: "These twelve men are believed which say that he was not born of fornication, but the whole multitude of us cry out that he was born of fornication, and is a sorcerer, and saith that he is the Son of God and a king, and we are not believed."

And Pilate commanded the whole multitude to go out, saving the twelve men which said that he was not born of fornication, and he commanded Jesus to be set apart: and Pilate saith unto them: "For what cause do they desire to put him to death?"

They say unto Pilate: "They have jealousy, because he healeth on the sabbath day."

Pilate saith: "For a good work do they desire to put him to death?"

They say unto him: "Yea."

And Pilate was filled with indignation and went forth without the judgement hall and saith unto them: "I call the Sun to witness that I find no fault in this man."

The Jews answered and said to the governor: "If this man

were not a malefactor we would not have delivered him unto thee."

And Pilate said: "Take ye him and judge him according to your law."

The Jews said unto Pilate: "It is not lawful for us to put any man to death."

Pilate said: "Hath God forbidden you to slay, and allowed me?"

And Pilate went in again into the judgement hall and called Jesus apart and said unto him: "Art thou the King of the Jews?"

Jesus answered and said to Pilate: "Sayest thou this thing of thyself, or did others tell it thee of me?"

Pilate answered Jesus: "Am I also a Jew? thine own nation and the chief priests have delivered thee unto me: what hast thou done?"

Jesus answered: "My kingdom is not of this world; for if my kingdom were of this world, my servants would have striven that I should not be delivered to the Jews . . ."

Pilate said unto him: "Art thou a king, then?"

Jesus answered him: "Thou sayest that I am a king; for this cause was I born and am come, that every one that is of the truth should hear my voice."

Pilate saith unto him: "What is truth?"

Jesus saith unto him: "Truth is of heaven."

Pilate saith: "Is there not truth upon earth?"

Jesus saith unto Pilate: "Thou seest how that they which speak the truth are judged of them that have authority upon earth."

And Pilate left Jesus in the judgement hall and went forth to the Jews and said unto them: "I find no fault in him."

The Jews say unto him: "This man said: 'I am able to destroy this temple and in three days to build it up.'"

Pilate saith: "What temple?"

The Jews say: "That which Solomon built in forty and six years, but which this man saith he will destroy and build it in three days."

Pilate saith unto them: "I am guiltless of the blood of this just man: see ye to it."

The Jews say: "His blood be upon us and on our children."

And Pilate called the elders and the priests and Levites unto him and said to them secretly: "Do not so: for there is nothing worthy of death whereof ye have accused him, for your accusation is concerning healing and profaning of the sabbath."

The elders and the priests and Levites say: "If a man blaspheme against Caesar, is he worthy of death or no?"

Pilate saith: "He is worthy of death."

The Jews say unto Pilate: "If a man be worthy of death if he blaspheme against Caesar, this man hath blasphemed against God."

Then the governor commanded all the Jews to go out from the judgement hall, and he called Jesus to him and saith unto him: "What shall I do with thee?"

Jesus saith unto Pilate: "Do as it hath been given thee."

Pilate saith: "How hath it been given?"

Jesus saith: "Moses and the prophets did foretell concerning my death and rising again."

Now the Jews inquired by stealth and heard, and they say unto Pilate: "What needest thou to hear further of this blasphemy?"

Pilate saith unto the Jews: "If this word be of blasphemy, take ye him for his blasphemy, and bring him into your synagogue and judge him according to your law."

The Jews say unto Pilate: "It is contained in our law, that if a man sin against a man, he is worthy to receive forty stripes save one: but he that blasphemeth against God, that he should be stoned with stoning."

Pilate saith unto them: "Take ye him and avenge yourselves of him in what manner ye will."

The Jews say unto Pilate: "We will that he be crucified."

Pilate saith: "He deserveth not to be crucified."

Now as the governor looked round about upon the multitude of the Jews which stood by, he beheld many of the Jews weeping, and said: "Not all the multitude desire that he should be put to death."

The elder of the Jews said: "To this end have the whole multitude of us come hither, that he should be put to death."

Pilate saith to the Jews: "Wherefore should he die?"

The Jews said: "Because he called himself the Son of God, and a king."

But a certain man, Nicodemus, a Jew, came and stood before the governor and said: "I beseech thee, good lord, bid me speak a few words."

Pilate saith: "Say on."

Nicodemus saith: "I said unto the elders and the priests and Levites and unto all the multitude of the Jews in the synagogue: 'Wherefore contend ye with this man? This man doeth many and wonderful signs, which no man hath done, neither will do: let him alone and contrive not any evil against him: if the signs which he doeth are of God, they will stand, but if they be of men, they will come to nought. For verily Moses, when he was sent of God into Egypt did many signs, which God commanded him to do before Pharaoh, king of Egypt; and there were there certain men, servants of Pharaoh, Jannes and Jambres, and they also did signs not a few, of them which Moses did, and the Egyptians held them as gods, even Jannes and Jambres: and whereas the signs which they did were not of God, they perished and those also that believed on them. And now let this man go, for he is not worthy of death.'"

The Jews say unto Nicodemus: "Thou didst become his disciple and thou speakest on his behalf."

Nicodemus saith unto them: "Is the governor also become his disciple, that he speaketh on his behalf? did not Caesar appoint him unto this dignity?"

And the Jews were raging and gnashing their teeth against Nicodemus. Pilate saith unto them: "Wherefore gnash ye your teeth against him, whereas ye have heard the truth?"

The Jews say unto Nicodemus: "Mayest thou receive his truth and his portion."

Nicodemus saith: "Amen, Amen: may I receive it as ye have said."

Now one of the Jews came forward and besought the governor that he might speak a word. The governor saith: "If thou wilt say aught, speak on."

And the Jew said: "Thirty and eight years lay I on a bed in suffering of pains, and at the coming of Jesus many that were possessed and laid with divers diseases were healed by him, and certain (faithful) young men took pity on me and carried me with my bed and brought me unto him; and when Jesus saw me he had compassion, and spake a word unto me: 'Take up thy bed and walk.' [See John 5:8.] And I took up my bed and walked."

The Jews say unto Pilate: "Ask of him what day it was whereon he was healed?"

Pilate said unto him that was healed of his sickness: "Tell me truly what day it was whereon he healed thee."

He that was healed saith: "On the sabbath."

The Jews say: "Did we not inform thee so, that upon the sabbath he healeth and casteth out devils?"

And another Jew came forward and said: "I was born blind: I heard words but I saw no man's face: and as Jesus passed by I cried with a loud voice: 'Have mercy on me, O son of David.' And he took pity on me and put his hands upon mine eyes and I received sight immediately."

And another Jew came forward and said: "I was bowed and he made me straight with a word."

And another said: "I was a leper, and he healed me with a word."

And a certain woman named Bernice crying out from afar off said: "I had an issue of blood and I touched the hem of his garment, and the flowing of my blood was stayed which I had twelve years."

The Jews say: "We have a law that a woman shall not come to give testimony."

And certain others, even a multitude both of men and

women, cried out, saying: "This man is a prophet and the devils are subject unto him."

Pilate saith to them . . . "Wherefore were not your teachers also subject unto him?"

They say unto Pilate: "We know not."

Others also said: "He raised up Lazarus which was dead out of his tomb after four days."

And the governor was afraid and said unto all the multitude of the Jews: "Wherefore will ye shed innocent blood?"

And he called unto him Nicodemus and those twelve men which said that he was not born of fornication, and said unto them: "What shall I do, for there riseth sedition among the people?"

They say unto him: "We know not; let them see to it."

Again Pilate called for all the multitude of the Jews and saith: "Ye know that ye have a custom that at the feast of unleavened bread I should release unto you a prisoner. Now I have a prisoner under condemnation in the prison, a murderer, Barabbas by name, and this Jesus also which standeth before you, in whom I find no fault: Whom will ye that I release unto you?"

But they cried out: "Barabbas."

Pilate saith: "What shall I do then with Jesus who is called Christ?"

The Jews say: "Let him be crucified."

But certain of the Jews answered: "Thou art not a friend of Caesar's if thou let this man go; for he called himself the Son of God and a king: thou wilt therefore have him for king and not Caesar."

And Pilate was wroth and said unto the Jews: "Your nation is always seditious and ye rebel against your benefactors."

The Jews say: "Against what benefactors?"

Pilate saith: "According as I have heard, your God brought you out of Egypt out of hard bondage, and led you safe through the sea as by dry land, and in the wilderness he nourished you with manna and gave you quails, and gave you water to drink out of a rock, and gave unto you a law. And in all these things ye provoked your God to anger, and sought out a molten calf, and angered your God and he sought to slay you: and Moses made supplication for you and ye were not put to death. And now ye do accuse me that I hate the king." And he rose up from the judgement-seat and sought to go forth.

And the Jews cried out, saying: "We know our king, even Caesar and not Jesus. For indeed the wise men brought gifts from the east unto him as unto a king, and when Herod heard from the wise men that a king was born, he sought to slay him; and when his father Joseph knew that, he took him and his mother and they fled into Egypt. And when Herod heard it he destroyed the children of the Hebrews that were born in Bethlehem."

And when Pilate heard these words he was afraid. And Pilate silenced the multitude, because they cried still, and said unto them: "So, then, this is he whom Herod sought?"

The Jews say: "Yea, this is he."

And Pilate took water and washed his hands before the sun, saying: "I am innocent of the blood of this just man: see ye to it."

Again the Jews cried out: "His blood be upon us and upon our children."

Then Pilate commanded the veil to be drawn before the judgement-seat whereon he sat, and saith into Jesus: "Thy nation hath convicted thee as being a king: therefore have I decreed that thou shouldest first be scourged according to the law of the pious emperors, and thereafter hanged upon the cross in the garden wherein thou wast taken: and let Dysmas and Gestas the two malefactors be crucified with thee."[3]

"... WAS CRUCIFIED, DIED, AND WAS BURIED ..."

The document now known to scholars as The Gospel of Peter, from which the following account of the crucifixion of Jesus was taken, was discovered in 1884 in a tomb at Akhmim, in Egypt, west of the Red Sea. Since it has been quoted by

writers in the second half of the second century it is believed
to have been written not later than A.D. 150. The writer seems
to have been familiar with the conventional gospels of the New
Testament, and to have produced the earliest account of the
passion that exists outside of the Bible.

Now there stood there Joseph the friend of Pilate and of the
Lord, and he, knowing that they were about to crucify him,
came unto Pilate and begged the body of Jesus for burial. And
Pilate sending unto Herod, begged his body. And Herod said:
"Brother Pilate, even if none had begged for him, we should
have buried him, since also the sabbath dawneth; for it is
written in the law that the sun should not set upon one that
hath been slain."

And he delivered him unto the people before the first day of
[or on the day before the] unleavened bread, even their feast.
And they having taken the Lord pushed him as they ran, and
said: "Let us hale the Son of God, now that we have gotten
authority over him."

And they put on him a purple robe, and made him sit upon
the seat of judgement, saying: "Give righteous judgement, thou
King of Israel."

And one of them brought a crown of thorns and set it upon
the Lord's head; and others stood and did spit in his eyes, and
others buffeted his cheeks; and others did prick him with a
reed, and some of them scourged him, saying: "With this honor
let us honor the son of God."

And they brought two malefactors, and crucified the Lord
betwixt them. But he kept silence, as one feeling no pain. And
when they set the cross upright, they wrote thereon: "This is
the King of Israel."

And they laid his garments before him, and divided them
among themselves and cast the lot upon them. But one of
those malefactors reproached them, saying: "We have thus
suffered for the evils which we have done; but this man which
hath become the saviour of men, wherein hath he injured you?"

And they were wroth with him, and commanded that his legs should not be broken, that so he might die in torment.

Now it was noonday, and darkness prevailed over all Judaea: and they were troubled and in an agony lest the sun should have set, for that he yet lived: for it is written for them that the sun should not set upon him that hath been slain. And one of them said: "Give ye him to drink gall with vinegar": and they mingled it and gave him to drink: and they fulfilled all things and accomplished their sins upon their own heads. And many went about with lamps, supposing that it was night: and some fell.

And the Lord cried out aloud saying: "My power, my power, thou hast forsaken me. . . ."

And in the same hour was the veil of the temple of Jerusalem rent in two. And then they plucked the nails from the hands of the Lord and laid him upon the earth: and the whole earth was shaken, and there came a great fear on all. Then the sun shone forth, and it was found to be the ninth hour. And the Jews rejoiced, and gave his body unto Joseph to bury it, because he had beheld all the good things which he did. And he took the Lord and washed him and wrapped him in linen and brought him unto his own sepulchre, which is called the Garden of Joseph.

Then the Jews and the elders and the priests, when they perceived how great evil they had done themselves, began to lament and say: "Woe unto our sins: the judgement and the end of Jerusalem is drawn nigh."

But I with my fellows was in grief, and we were wounded in our minds and would have hid ourselves; for we were sought after by them as malefactors, and as thinking to set the temple on fire. And beside all these things we were fasting, and we sat mourning and weeping night and day until the sabbath.

But the scribes and Pharisees and elders gathered one with another, for they had heard that all the people were murmuring and beating their breasts, saying: "If these very great signs have come to pass at his death, behold how righteous he was."

And the elders were afraid and came unto Pilate, entreating him and saying: "Give us soldiers that we may watch his sepulchre for three days, lest his disciples come and steal him away and the people suppose that he is risen from the dead, and do us hurt."

And Pilate gave them Petronius the centurion with soldiers to watch the sepulchre; and the elders and scribes came with them unto the tomb, and when they had rolled a great stone to keep out the centurion and the soldiers, then all that were there together set it upon the door of the tomb; and plastered thereon seven seals; and they pitched a tent there and kept watch.

And early in the morning as the sabbath dawned, there came a multitude from Jerusalem and the region round about to see the sepulchre that had been sealed.[4]

6

THE RESURRECTION

JESUS APPEARS TO JOHN

*The following is from a manuscript probably of the middle of
the second century known as The Acts of John. The beginning
of it is lost, but it was apparently originally about as long as
the Gospel according to Matthew. The John referred to in the
title was the disciple John and not John the Baptist. This is the
same manuscript as that from which the second selection under
the heading "Prelude to Suffering" was taken. John is speaking:*

I, then, when I saw him suffer, did not even abide by his
suffering, but fled unto the Mount of Olives, weeping at that
which had befallen. And when he was crucified on the Friday,
at the sixth hour of the day, darkness came upon all the earth.

And my Lord standing in the midst of the cave and enlightening it, said: "John, unto the multitude below in Jerusalem I am
being crucified and pierced with lances and reeds, and gall and
vinegar is given me to drink. But unto thee I speak, and what I
speak hear thou. I put it into thy mind to come up into this
mountain, that thou mightest hear those things which it behoveth a disciple to learn from his teacher and a man from his
God."

And having thus spoken, he showed me a cross of light fixed
and therein was one form and one likeness: and in the cross
another multitude, not having one form. And the Lord himself
I beheld above the cross, not having any shape, but only a

voice: and a voice not such as familiar to us, but one sweet and kind and truly of God, saying unto me: "John, it is needful that one should hear these things from me, for I have need of one that will hear. This cross of light is sometimes called the word by me for your sakes, sometimes mind, sometimes Jesus, sometimes Christ, sometimes door, sometimes a way, sometimes bread, sometimes seed, sometimes resurrection, sometimes Son, sometimes Father, sometimes Spirit, sometimes life, sometimes truth, sometimes faith, sometimes grace. And by these names it is called as toward men: but that which it is in truth, as conceived of in itself and as spoken of unto you it is the marking-off of all things, and the firm uplifting of things fixed out of things unstable, and the harmony of wisdom, and indeed wisdom in harmony. There are places of the right hand and the left, powers also, authorities, lordships and demons, workings, threatenings, wraths, devils, Satan, and the lower root whence the nature of the things that come into being proceeded.

"This cross, then, is that which fixed all things apart by the word, and separated off the things that are from those that are below and then also, being one, streamed forth into all things. But this is not the cross of wood which thou wilt see when thou goest down hence: neither am I he that is on the cross, whom now thou seest not, but only hearest his voice. I was reckoned to be that which I am not, not being what I was unto many others: but they will call me something else which is vile and not worthy of me. As, then, the place of rest is neither seen nor spoken of, much more shall I, the Lord thereof, be neither seen nor spoken of.

"Now the multitude of one aspect that is about the cross is the lower nature: and they whom thou seest in the cross, if they have not one form, it is because not yet hath every member of him that came down been comprehended. But when the human nature is taken up, and the race which draweth near unto me and obeyeth my voice, he that now heareth me shall be united therewith, and shall no more be that which now he is, but above them, as I also now am. For so long as thou callest not thyself mine, I am not that which I am; but if thou hear me, thou, hearing, shalt be as I am, and I shall be that which I was, when I have thee as I am with myself. For from me thou art that which I am. Care not therefore for the many, and them that are outside the mystery despise; for know thou that I am wholly with the Father, and the Father with me.

"Nothing, therefore, of the things which they will say of me have I suffered: nay, that suffering also which I showed unto thee and the rest in the dance, I will that it be called a mystery. For what thou art, thou seest, for I showed it thee; but what I am I alone know, and no man else. Suffer me then to keep that which is mine, and that which is thine behold thou through me, and behold me in truth, that I am, not what I said, but what thou art able to know, because thou art akin thereto. Thou hearest that I suffered, yet did I not suffer; that I suffered not, yet did I suffer; that I was pierced, yet I was not smitten; hanged, and I was not hanged; that blood flowed from me, and it flowed not; and, in a word, what they say of me, that befell me not, but what they say not, that did I suffer. Now what those things are I signify unto thee, for I know that thou wilt understand. Perceive thou therefore in me the praising of the Word (Logos), the piercing of the Word, the blood of the Word, the wound of the Word, the hanging up of the Word, the suffering of the Word, the nailing of the Word, the death of the Word. And so speak I, separating off the manhood. Perceive thou therefore in the first place of the Word; then shalt thou perceive the Lord, and in the third place the man, and what he hath suffered."[1]

THE ACCOUNT OF JOSEPH OF ARIMATHAEA

The following is one of a group of manuscripts which scholars consider fictional, and, in the case of this one, very late—possibly of the twelfth century.

I, Joseph of Arimathaea, who begged the body of the Lord Jesus from Pilate, was imprisoned by the Jews on that account.

These are the people who provoked their lawgiver Moses, and, failing to recognize their God, crucified his Son.

Seven days before the passion of Christ, two condemned robbers were sent from Jericho to Pilate, whose crimes were these: The first, Gestas, used to strip and murder wayfarers, hang up women by the feet and cut off their breasts, drink the blood of babes: he knew not God nor obeyed any law, but was violent from the beginning.

The other, Demas, was a Galilaean who kept an inn; he despoiled the rich but did good to the poor, even burying them, like Tobit. He had committed robberies on the Jews, for he stole the law itself at Jerusalem, and stripped the daughter of Caiaphas, who was a priestess of the sanctuary, and he took away even the mystic deposit of Solomon which had been deposited in the holy place.

Jesus also was taken at even on the third day before the passover. But Caiaphas and the multitude of the Jews had no passover but were in great grief because of the robbery of the sanctuary by the thief. And they sent for Judas Iscariot who was brother's son to Caiaphas, and had been persuaded by the Jews to become a disciple of Jesus, not to follow his teachings, but to betray him. They paid him a didrachm of gold daily; and as one of Jesus' disciples, called John, says, he had been two years with Jesus.

On the third day before Jesus was taken, Judas said to the Jews: "Let us assemble a council and say that it was not the robber who took away the law, but Jesus."

Nicodemus, who had the keys of the sanctuary, said "No": for he was a truthful man.

But Sarra, Caiaphas' daughter, cried out that Jesus said in public, "I can destroy the temple." All the Jews said: "We believe you." For they held her as a prophetess. So Jesus was taken.

On the morrow, being Wednesday, at the ninth hour, they brought him into Caiaphas' hall, and Annas and Caiaphas asked him: "Why didst thou take away the law?" He was silent.

"Why wouldst thou destroy the temple of Solomon?" He was silent.

In the evening the multitude sought the daughter of Caiaphas, to burn her with fire, because the law was stolen and they could not keep the passover. But she said: "Wait a little, my children, and let us destroy Jesus, and the law will be found and the feast kept."

Then Annas and Caiaphas privily gave gold to Judas and said: "Say as you said before, that it was Jesus who stole the law."

Judas agreed, but said: "The people must not know that you have told me this: and you must let Jesus go, and I will persuade them." So they fraudulently let Jesus go.

At dawn of the Thursday Judas went into the sanctuary and said to all the people: "What will ye give me if I deliver to you the destroyer of the law and robber of the prophets?"

They said: "Thirty pieces of gold." But they did not know that it was Jesus of whom he spoke, for many thought him to be the Son of God. And Judas received the thirty pieces.

At the fourth and fifth hours he went out and found Jesus walking in the street. Toward evening he obtained a guard of soldiers. As they went, Judas said: "Whomsoever I shall kiss, take him: he it is that stole the law and the prophets."

He came to Jesus and kissed him, saying: "Hail, Rabbi."

They took Jesus to Caiaphas and examined him. "Why didst thou do this?" but he answered nothing. . . .

They did many evil things to Jesus that night, and on the dawn of Friday delivered him to Pilate. He was condemned and crucified with the two robbers, Gestas on the left, Demas on the right.

He on the left cried out to Jesus: "See what evils I have wrought on the earth; and had I known thou wert the king, I would have killed thee too. Why callest thou thyself Son of God and canst not help thyself in the hour of need? Or how canst thou succour any other that prayeth? if thou be the Christ, come down from the cross that I may believe thee. But now I behold thee, not as a man but as a wild beast caught and perishing along with me." And much else he spake against Jesus, blaspheming and gnashing his teeth upon him: for he was caught in the snare of the devil.

But Demas, on the right, seeing the divine grace of Jesus, began to cry out thus: "I know thee, Jesus Christ, that thou art the Son of God. I see thee, Christ, worshipped by ten thousand times ten thousand angels; forgive my sins that I have committed: make not the stars to enter into judgement with me, or the moon, when thou judgest all the world: for in the night did I work my evil plans: stir not up the sun that now is darkened for thy sake to tell the evil of my heart: for I can give thee no gift for remission of sins. Already death cometh on me for my sins, but pardon belongeth unto thee: save me, Lord of all things, from thy terrible judgement: give not power unto the enemy to swallow me up and be inheritor of my soul, as of his that hangeth on the left; for I see how the devil taketh his soul rejoicing, and his flesh vanisheth away. Neither command me to depart into the lot of the Jews, for I see Moses and the patriarchs weeping sore, and the devil exulting over them. Therefore before my spirit departeth, command O Lord that my sins be blotted out, and remember me the sinner in thy kingdom when thou sittest on the great throne of the Most High and shalt judge the twelve tribes of Israel: for thou hast prepared great punishment for thy world for thy sake."

And when the thief had so said, Jesus saith unto him: "Verily, verily, I say unto thee, Demas, that to-day thou shalt be with me in paradise: but the sons of the kingdom, the children of Abraham, Isaac, and Jacob, and Moses shall be cast out into the outer darkness: there shall be weeping and gnashing of teeth. But thou only shalt dwell in paradise until my second coming, when I shall judge them that have not confessed my name. . . . Go and say unto the cherubim and the powers that turn about the flaming sword, that keep the garden since Adam the first-created was in paradise and transgressed and kept not my commandments and I cast him out thence—but none of the former men shall see paradise until I come the second time to judge the quick and dead—"

And he wrote thus: "Jesus Christ the Son of God that came down from the heights of heaven, that proceeded out of the bosom of the invisible Father without separation, and came down into the world to be incarnate and to be nailed to the cross, that I might save Adam whom I formed: unto my powers the archangels, that keep the doors of paradise, the servants of my Father: I will and command that he that is crucified with me receive remission of his sins for my sake, and being clothed with an incorruptible body enter in to paradise, and that he dwell there where no man else is ever able to dwell."

And when this was said, Jesus gave up the ghost on Friday at the ninth hour. And there was darkness over all the land and a great earthquake, so that the sanctuary fell, and the pinnacle of the temple.

And I, Joseph, begged the body and laid it in my new tomb. The body of Demas was not found: that of Gestas was in appearance like that of a dragon.

The Jews imprisoned me on the evening of the sabbath.

When it was evening on the first day of the week, at the fifth hour of the night, Jesus came to me with the thief on the right hand. There was great light; the house was raised up by the four corners and I went forth: and I perceived Jesus first, and then the thief bringing a letter to him, and as we journeyed to Galilee there was a very great light, and a sweet fragrance came from the thief. . . .

And as I went with Jesus and the robber to Galilee, the form of Jesus was changed and he became wholly light, and angels ministered to him and he conversed with them. I stayed with him three days, and none of the disciples were there.[2]

JUDAS AND THE COCK

The Acts of Pilate, also known as The Gospel of Nicodemus, from which the first of the two following selections is taken, is

*an obscure work the origin of which is unknown. Bits of it are
known in Greek, Latin, Coptic, Syriac, and Armenian. The
earliest form of it is believed to have been written as late as the
fourth century.*

Departing to his house to make a halter of rope to hang
himself, he [Judas] found his wife sitting and roasting a cock
on a fire of coals or in a pan before eating it: and saith to her:
"Rise up, wife, and provide me a rope, for I would hang myself,
as I deserve."

But his wife said to him: "Why sayest thou such things?"

And Judas saith to her: "Know of a truth that I have wickedly
betrayed my master Jesus to the evil-doers for Pilate to put him
to death: but he will rise again on the third day, and woe unto
us!"

And his wife said to him: "Say not nor think not so: for as well
as this cock that is roasting on the fire of coals can crow, just so
well shall Jesus rise again, as thou sayest." And immediately at
her word that cock spread his wings and crowed thrice.

Then was Judas yet more convinced, and straightway made
the halter of rope and hanged himself.[3]

*Another narrative of Judas and the cock follows. Little is
known of its source. M. R. James simply says that it is from the
Ethiopic "Book of the Cock" which is read in the Abyssinian
church every Maundy Thursday.*

Akrosina, the wife of Simon the Pharisee, brought a cock cut
up with a knife, put it in a magnificent dish, and set it on the
table before our Lord.

Jesus said, "My time is at hand." He blessed the bread and
gave it to Judas. Satan entered into him and he went out—
without receiving the blessing of Jesus.

Jesus touched the slain cock and it stood up whole. He bade it
follow Judas and see what he did, and return and report it:

he endowed it with human speech. It followed Judas home: his wife urged him to betray Jesus. He went to the temple. The dialogue with the Jews is reported, and Paul of Tarsus, "son of Josue Almason, son of Cadafanâ," a rough man, says, "Now, thou, deliver him into my hands without error."

The cock returned to Bethany, and sat before Jesus and wept bitterly, and told all the story. The disciples wept. Jesus dismissed the cock to mount up into the sky for a thousand years.[4]

". . . HE DESCENDED INTO HELL . . ."

At this point the chronolgy of the apocryphal stories becomes somewhat confused. In the creed the descent into hell precedes the resurrection, and indeed in the best apocryphal version of the resurrection, when Jesus emerges from the tomb a question asked by "a voice" and the answer made by Jesus seem to indicate that he has been in hell and has returned from there. Yet between the crucifixion and the descent into hell, there are several appearances of Jesus to one or more of the disciples. The chronology followed here is that indicated by the creed.

And he . . . sat in the midst of them. But they doubted to question him, being afraid. And Jesus . . . said unto them: "Ask me what ye will that I should teach you, and I will show it you." . . .

But they, yet doubting, said unto him: "Lord, show us the deep (abyss) according unto thy promise."

And Jesus said unto them: "It is not good for you to see the deep: notwithstanding, if ye desire it, according to my promise, come, follow me and behold."

And he led them away into a place that is called Cherubim, that is the place of truth. And he beckoned unto the angels of the West, and the earth was rolled up like a volume of a book and the deep was revealed unto them. And when the apostles saw it, they fell on their faces upon the earth. But Jesus raised them up, saying: "Said I not unto you, 'It is not good for you to see the deep'?"

And again he beckoned unto the angels, and the deep was covered up. . . .

Now when they came up to the top of the mount . . . the Master was withdrawn from them a little space . . . When Jesus appeared again, Bartholomew saith unto him: "Lord, show us the adversary of men that we may behold him, of what fashion he is, and what is his work, and whence he cometh forth, and what power he hath that he spared not even thee, but caused thee to be hanged upon the tree."

But Jesus looked upon him and said: "Thou bold heart! thou askest for that which thou art not able to look upon."

But Bartholomew was troubled and fell at Jesus' feet and began to speak thus: "O lamp that cannot be quenched, Lord Jesu Christ, maker of the eternal light, that hast given unto them that love thee the grace that beautifieth all, and hast given us the eternal light by thy coming into the world, that hast . . . accomplished the work of the Father, hast turned the shame-facedness of Adam into mirth, hast done away the sorrow of Eve with a cheerful countenance by thy birth from a virgin: remember not evil against me but grant me the word of mine asking."

And as he thus spake, Jesus raised him up and said unto him: "Bartholomew, wilt thou see the adversary of men? I tell thee that when thou beholdest him, not thou only but the rest of the apostles and Mary will fall on your faces and become as dead corpses."

But they all said unto him: "Lord, let us behold him."

And he led them down . . . and looked wrathfully upon the angels that keep hell and beckoned unto Michael to sound the trumpet in the height of the heavens. And Michael sounded, and the earth shook, and Beliar* came up, being held by 660

---

* A variant of "Belial," a name used for the personification of wickedness in the OT and by Paul in II Cor. 6:15, to mean Satan.

angels and bound with fiery chains. And the length of him was 1,600 cubits and his breadth 40 cubits and his face was like a lightning of fire and his eyes full of darkness. And out of his nostrils came a stinking smoke; and his mouth was as the gulf of a precipice, and the one of his wings was four-score cubits.

And straightway when the apostles saw him, they fell to the earth on their faces and became as dead. But Jesus came near and raised the apostles and gave them a spirit of power, and he saith unto Bartholomew: "Come near, Bartholomew, and trample *with* thy feet on his neck, and he will tell thee his work, what it is, and how he deceiveth men." And Jesus stood afar off with the rest of the apostles.

And Bartholomew feared, and raised his voice and said: "Blessed be the name of thine immortal kingdom from henceforth even for ever."

And when he had spoken, Jesus permitted him, *saying:* "Go and tread upon the neck of Beliar": and Bartholomew ran quickly upon him and trod upon his neck: and Beliar trembled.

And Bartholomew was afraid, and fled, and said unto Jesus: "Lord, give me an hem of thy garments that I may have courage to draw near unto him."

But Jesus said unto him: "Thou canst not take an hem of my garments, for these are not my garments which I wore before I was crucified."

And Bartholomew said: "Lord, I fear lest, like as he spared not thine angels, he swallow me up also."

Jesus saith unto him: "Were not all things made by my word, and by the will of my Father the spirits were made subject unto Solomon? Thou, therefore, being commanded by my word, go in my name and ask him what thou wilt."

And Bartholomew went and trod upon his neck, and pressed down his face into the earth as far as his ears, and . . . saith unto him: "Tell me who thou art and what is thy name."

And he [Beliar] said to him: "Lighten me a little, and I will tell thee who I am and how I came hither, and what my work is and what my power is."

And he lightened him and saith to him: "Say all that thou hast done and all that thou doest."

And Beliar said: "If thou wilt know my name, at the first I was called Satanael, which is interpreted a messenger of God, but when I rejected the image of God my name was called Satanas, that is, an angel that keepeth hell."

And again Bartholomew saith unto him: "Reveal unto me all things and hide nothing from me."

And he said unto him: "I swear unto thee by the power of the glory of God that even if I would hide aught I cannot, for he is near that would convict me. For if I were able I would have destroyed you like one of them that were before you. For, indeed, I was formed the first angel: for when God made the heavens, he took a handful of fire and formed me first, Michael second so that we also were created by the will of the Son and the consent of the Father. He formed, *I say*, first me, next Michael the chief captain of the hosts that are above, Gabriel third, Uriel fourth, Raphael fifth, Nathanael sixth, and other angels of whom I cannot tell the names.

"For they are the rod-bearers of God, and they smite me with their rods and pursue me seven times in the night and seven times in the day, and leave me not at all and break in pieces all my power.

"These are the angels of vengeance which stand before the throne of God: these are the angels that were first formed. And after them were formed all the angels. . . . But the rest I will not tell thee, for he that standeth by suffereth me not."

Bartholomew saith unto him: "How chastisest thou the souls of men?"

Beliar saith unto him: "Wilt thou that I declare unto thee the punishment of the hypocrites, of the back-biters, of the jesters, of the idolaters, and the covetous, and the adulterers, and the wizards, and the diviners, and of them that believe in us, and of all whom I look upon?"

Bartholomew said unto him: "Declare quickly how thou persuadest men not to follow God, and thine evil arts, that are slippery and dark, that they should leave the straight and shining paths of the Lord. . . . I will that thou declare it in few words."

And he [Beliar] smote his teeth together, gnashing them, and there came up out of the bottomless pit a wheel having a sword flashing with fire, and in the sword were pipes. And [Bartholomew] asked him: "What is this sword?"

And he said: "This sword is the sword of the gluttonous: for into this pipe are sent they that through their gluttony devise all manner of sin; into the second pipe are sent the backbiters which backbite their neighbour secretly; into the third pipe are sent the hypocrites and the rest whom I overthrow by my contrivance."

And Bartholomew said: "Dost thou then do these things by thyself alone?"

And Satan said: "If I were able to go forth by myself, I would have destroyed the whole world in three days: but neither I nor any of the six hundred go forth. For we have other swift ministers whom we command, and we furnish them with an hook of many points and send them forth to hunt, and they catch for us souls of men, enticing them with sweetness of divers baits, that is by drunkenness and laughter, by backbiting, hypocrisy, pleasures, fornication, and the rest of the trifles that come out of their treasures." . . .

Bartholomew saith unto him: "Be still and be faint, that I may entreat my Lord."

And he fell upon his face and cast earth upon his head and said, "O Lord Jesu Christ, the great and glorious name. All the choirs of the angels praise thee, O Master, and I that am unworthy with my lips do praise thee, O Master. Hearken unto me thy servant, and as thou didst choose me from the receipt of custom and didst not suffer me to have my conversation unto the end in my former deeds, O Lord Jesu Christ, hearken unto me and have mercy upon the sinners."

And when he had so said, the Lord saith unto him: "Rise up, suffer him that groaneth *to arise:* I will declare the rest unto thee."

And Bartholomew raised up Satan and said unto him: "Go unto thy place, with thine angels; but the Lord hath mercy upon all his world."

But the devil said: "Suffer me, and I will tell thee how I was cast down into this place and how the Lord did make man. I was going to and fro in the world, and God said unto Michael: 'Bring me a clod from the four corners of the earth, and water out of the four rivers of paradise.'

"And when Michael brought them God formed Adam in the regions of the east, and shaped the clod which was shapeless, and stretched sinews and veins *upon it* and established it with joints; and he worshipped him, himself for his own sake first, because he was the image of God, therefore he worshipped him. And when I came from the ends of the earth Michael said: 'Worship thou the image of God, which he hath made according to his likeness.'

"But I said: 'I am fire of fire, I was the first angel formed, and shall I worship clay and matter?'

"And Michael saith to me: 'Worship, lest God be wroth with thee.' But I said to him: 'God will not be wroth with me; but I will set my throne over against his throne, and I will be as he is.'

"Then was God wroth with me and cast me down, having commanded the windows of heaven to be opened. And when I was cast down, he asked also the six hundred that were under me, if they would worship: but they said: 'Like as we have seen the first angel do, neither will we worship him that is less than ourselves.'

"Then were the six hundred also cast down by him with me. And when we were cast down upon the earth we were senseless for forty years; and when the sun shone forth seven times brighter than fire, suddenly I awaked; and I looked about and saw the six hundred that were under me senseless.

"And I awaked my son Salpsan and took him to counsel how I might deceive the man on whose account I was cast out of the heavens. And thus did I contrive it. I took a vial in mine hand and scraped the sweat from off my breast and the hair of mine armpits, and washed myself in the springs of the waters whence the four rivers flow out, and Eve drank of it and desire came upon her: for if she had not drunk of that water I should not have been able to deceive her."

Then Bartholomew commanded him to go into hell. . . .

Then I, Bartholomew, which wrote these things in mine heart, took hold on the hand of the Lord the lover of men and began to rejoice and to speak thus:

"Glory be to thee, O Lord Jesus Christ, that givest unto all thy grace which all we have perceived. Alleluia.

"Glory be to thee, O Lord, the life of sinners.

"Glory be to thee, O Lord, death is put to shame.

"Glory be to thee, O Lord, the treasure of righteousness.

"For unto God do we sing."

And as Bartholomew thus spake again, Jesus put off his mantle and took a kerchief from the neck of Bartholomew and began to rejoice and said: "I am good: mild and gracious and merciful, strong and righteous, wonderful and holy: I am good. Alleluia. I am meek and gentle. Alleluia. Glory be to thee, O Lord: for I give gifts unto all them that desire me. Alleluia.

"Glory be to thee, O Lord, world without end. Amen. Alleluia."

And when he had ceased, the apostles kissed him, and he gave them the peace of love.[5]

THE TESTIMONY OF KARINUS

For this vivid account of the descent into hell and the resurrection we are indebted, as we are for other stories, to the Acts of Pilate, of unknown authorship. Apparently it was written, in the form of an eyewitness account, to furnish evidence of the resurrection, thus denying the statements of unbelievers. How

*successful it is in that mission is for anyone's judgment to decide.
It is, in any case, a graphic and attention-holding story.*

And behold on a sudden there appeared coming down from
Mount Amalech a very great multitude, about twelve thousand
men, which had risen with the Lord. And though the men
recognized many in that place, they were not able to speak a
word unto them because of their fear, and the vision of angels;
and they stood afar off beholding them and hearkening to them,
how they went singing and saying: "The Lord is risen from the
dead as he said: let us all rejoice and be glad, for he reigneth for
ever."

Then they that had been sent were amazed and fell down
upon the earth for fear: and they were warned by an angel
of the Lord which raised them up from the earth, that they
should seek out Karinus and Leucius in their own house.

They arose then and went to their house and found them
giving themselves unto prayer: and entering in unto them they
fell on their faces to the earth and greeted them, and arose
and said: "O ye friends of God, the whole multitude of the
Jews hath sent us unto you, for they have heard that ye are
risen from the dead, entreating and beseeching you to come unto
them, that we may all know the wonderful works of God which
have been wrought upon us in our days." And they . . . went
with them, and entered into their synagogue. And when the
chief of the priests saw them they were greatly troubled and
trembling took hold upon them: and finally Annas and Caiaphas
took the books of the law of God and put them into their hands,
and adjured them by the god Heloi and the god Adonai and by
the law and the prophets, saying: "Tell us how ye arose from
the dead, and what are these wonders which have been wrought
in our days, even such as we have never heard to be done at
any time: for now all our bones are confounded and dried up
for fear, and the earth moveth itself beneath our feet: for verily
we have joined together all our hearts to shed righteous and
holy blood."

Then Karinus and Leucius beckoned to them with their hands that they should give them a volume of paper, and ink: and this they did because the Holy Ghost suffered them not to speak with them. And they gave unto each of them paper, and separated them one from the other in several chambers. And they, making with their fingers the sign of the cross of Christ, began to write each his volume; and when they had ended, they cried out as it were with one voice out of their several chambers: "Amen." And Karinus rose and gave his paper unto Annas and Leucius unto Caiaphas. . . .

Then Annas and Caiaphas opened the roll of paper and began each of them to read to himself privily. But all the people took it ill, and there was a cry from all of them: "Read these writings unto us openly: and when they have been read, we will keep them, that this truth of God be not turned by blinding our eyes, unto deceit, by unclean and deceitful men."

And thereupon Annas and Caiaphas, being seized with trembling, delivered the roll of paper unto Rabbi Addas and Rabbi Fineës and Rabbi Egias. . . . And they read the paper, wherein was contained this that followeth:

I Karinus. O Lord Jesu Christ, son of the living God, suffer me to speak of thy marvellous works which thou didst in hell.

When therefore we were holden in hell in darkness and the shadow of death, suddenly there shone upon us a great light, and hell did tremble, and the gates of death. And there was heard the voice of the Son of the most high Father, as it were the voice of a great thundering, and it proclaimed aloud and began: "Draw back, O princes, your gates, remove your everlasting doors: Christ the Lord the king of glory approacheth to enter in."

Then came Satan the prince of death, fleeing in fear and saying to his ministers and unto the hells: "O my ministers and all the hells, come together, and shut your gates, set in place the bars of iron, and fight boldly and withstand, that we that hold them be not made captive in bonds."

Then were all his evil ministers troubled, and began to shut

the gates of death with all diligence, and by little to make fast
the locks and the bars of iron, and to take fast in hand all their
instruments, and to utter howlings with dreadful and hideous
voice.

Then said Satan unto Hell: "Make thee ready to receive him
whom I shall bring down unto thee."

Thereupon did Hell make answer unto Satan thus: "This voice
was nothing else but the cry of the Son of the most high Father,
that the earth and all the places of hell did so quake at it: wherefore I think that I and all my bonds are now wide open. But I
adjure thee, O Satan, head of all evil, by thy might and mine
own, bring him not unto me, lest when we would take him we
be taken captive of him. For if by his voice only all my might
hath been thus overthrown, what, thinkest thou, will he do when
his presence is come unto us?" . . .

Now the saints of God heard the contention between Satan
and Hell: but as yet they knew not each other among themselves:
nevertheless they were at the point to know. But our holy father
Adam made answer unto Satan thus: "O prince of death, wherefore fearest thou and tremblest? Behold the Lord cometh which
shall destroy all thy creatures, and thou shalt be taken captive of
him and be bound, world without end."

Then all the saints, when they heard the voice of our father
Adam, how valiantly he made answer unto Satan, were glad
and were comforted: and all of them ran together unto father
Adam and were gathered about him in that place. Then our
father Adam, looking earnestly upon all that multitude, marvelled if they all were begotten of him into the world. And he
embraced them that stood near round about him, and shed exceeding bitter tears, and spake unto Seth his son: "Declare, my
son Seth, unto the holy patriarchs and prophets that which the
keeper of paradise said unto thee when I sent thee to bring me of
the very oil of mercy that thou mightest anoint my body when
I was sick."

Then he answered: "I, when thou sentest me before the gates
of paradise, prayed and besought the Lord with tears, and I

called the keeper of paradise to give me thereof. Then Michael the archangel came forth and said unto me: Seth, wherefore mournest thou? know thou before, that thy father Adam shall not receive of this oil of mercy now, but after many generations of the world. For the most beloved Son of God shall come down from heaven into the world and shall be baptized of John in the river Jordan: and then shall thy father Adam receive of this oil of mercy, and all they that believe in him: and the kingdom of them which have believed in him shall endure, world without end."

Then all the saints when they heard these things rejoiced again with great joy, and one of them that stood by, Isaias by name, proclaimed with a loud voice, saying: "Father Adam and all ye that stand by hearken unto my sayings. While I was upon earth, and the Holy Ghost taught me, I did sing in prophecy concerning this light, saying: 'The people which sat in darkness have seen a great light: unto them which dwell in the land of the shadow of death hath the light shined.'" [Isaiah 9:2.]

And at his word Father Adam and they all turned unto him and asked him: "Who art thou?" for that which thou sayest is true.

And he answered and said: "I am named Isaias."

Then appeared there another beside him, as it were a dweller in the wilderness, and they asked him and said: "Who art thou that bearest in thy body such signs?" and he answered stoutly: "I am John the Baptist, the voice and the prophet of the Most High. I went before the face of the same Lord to make the desert and rough ways into plain paths. I did show with my finger unto them of Jerusalem the lamb of the Lord and the Son of God, and glorified him. I baptized him in the river Jordan. I heard the voice of the Father out of heaven thundering upon him and proclaiming: 'This is my beloved Son in whom I am well pleased.' I have received an answer from him that he would himself descend into hell."

Then Father Adam, when he heard that, cried with a loud

voice, and shouted again and again "Alleluia," which is, being interpreted: "The Lord cometh."

After this another that stood by and was adorned as it were
with the marks of an emperor, by name David, cried out thus
and said: "When I was upon earth I did reveal unto the people
concerning the mercy of God and his visitation, and prophesied
joyful things to come throughout all ages, saying: 'Let them give
thanks unto the Lord, even his mercies: and his wonders unto
the children of men. For he hath broken the gates of brass and
smitten the bars of iron in sunder.'"

Then did the holy patriarchs and prophets begin to recognize
one another, and each one of them to speak words out of their
prophecies. Then holy Jeremias, looking upon his prophecies,
said to the patriarchs and prophets: "When I was upon earth I
prophesied of the Son of God, *saying* that he was seen upon
earth and conversed among men."

Then all the saints rejoicing in the light of the Lord and at
the sight of their father Adam, and at the answer of all the patriarchs and prophets, cried out, saying: "Alleluia, blessed is he that
cometh in the name of the Lord."

So that at the cry of them Satan feared, and sought a way to
flee by, and could not, for Hell and his ministers did hold him
bound in hell and fenced in on every side.

And they said unto him: "Why fearest thou? we will in no wise
suffer thee to go out hence; but thou must receive these things
as thou art worthy, at his hands whom thou didst fight against
every day: and if not, know thou that thou shalt be bound by
him and committed unto my keeping for ever."

And again there came the voice of the Son of the most high
Father, as the voice of a great thunder, saying: "Lift up, O
princes, your gates, and be ye lift up, ye everlasting doors, and
the King of glory shall come in."

Then Satan and Hell cried out, saying: "Who is this King of
glory?"

And it was answered them by the Lord's voice: "The Lord
strong and mighty, the Lord mighty in battle." [Psalm 24:8.]

After that voice there came unto us a man whose appearance was as that of a robber, bearing a cross upon his shoulder, who cried without and said: "Open unto me that I may enter in."

And Satan opened the gate unto him a little way and brought him within the house, and shut the gate again after him. And all the saints saw him that he shone brightly, and said unto him straightway: "Thine appearance is that of a robber: show us, what is that which thou bearest on thy back?"

And he answered humbly and said: "Of a truth I was a robber altogether, and the Jews hanged me upon a cross with my Lord Jesus Christ, the Son of the most high Father. And at the last I have come hither before him; but himself cometh after me immediately."

Then the holy David's anger was kindled against Satan, and he cried aloud: "Open, thou most foul one, thy gates, that the King of glory may come in."

Likewise also all the saints of God rose up against Satan and would have laid hold on him and parted him among them.

And again there was a cry without: "Lift up, ye princes, your gates, and be ye lift up, ye everlasting doors, and the King of glory shall come in." [Psalm 24:7.]

And again at that clear voice Hell and Satan inquired, saying: "Who is this King of glory?" and it was said unto them by that marvellous voice: "The Lord of hosts, he is the King of glory." [Psalm 24:10.]

And lo, suddenly Hell did quake, and the gates of death and the locks were broken small, and the bars of iron broken, and fell to the ground, and all things were laid open. And Satan remained in the midst and stood put to confusion and cast down, and bound with a fetter about his feet. And behold, the Lord Jesus Christ coming in the glory of the light of the height, in meekness, great and yet humble, bearing a chain in his hands bound therewith the neck of Satan, and also, binding his hands behind his back, cast him backward into Tartarus, and set his holy foot upon his throat and said: "Throughout all ages hast thou done much evil and hast never been quiet at any time. To-day do I deliver thee unto eternal fire." And he called Hell quickly and gave him commandment, saying: "Take this most evil and wicked one and hold him in thy keeping until that day when I shall command thee." And he took him from beneath the Lord's feet, and he was cast down together with him into the depth of the bottomless pit.

Then the Lord Jesus, the Saviour of all men, pitiful and most gracious, greeted Adam with kindness, saying unto him: "Peace be unto thee, Adam, and unto thy children unto everlasting ages. Amen."

Then Father Adam cast himself at the Lord's feet, and rose up and kissed his hands, and shed abundant tears, saying: "Behold the hands which formed me: testifying unto all. . . . Thou art come, O King of glory, to set men free and gather them to thine everlasting kingdom."

Then our mother Eve also in like manner cast herself at the feet of the Lord, and rose up and kissed his hands, and shed tears abundantly, and said: "Behold the hands which fashioned me: testifying unto all."

Then all the saints adoring him cried out, saying: "Blessed is he that cometh in the name of the Lord: God the Lord hath showed us light. Amen throughout all ages. Alleluia, world without end: laud, honour, might, and glory, because thou hast come from on high to visit us." And they gathered them beneath the hands of the Lord, singing always Alleluia, and rejoicing together at the glory. . . .

Then all the saints of God besought the Lord that he would leave the sign of victory—even of the holy cross—in hell, that the wicked ministers thereof might not prevail to keep back any that was accused, whom the Lord absolved. And so it was done, and the Lord set his cross in the midst of hell, which is the sign of victory; and it shall remain there for ever.

Then all we went out thence with the Lord, and left Satan and Hell in Tartarus.

But unto us and many others was it commanded that we should rise again with our bodies, and bear witness in the world

of the resurrection of our Lord Jesus Christ, and concerning those
things that were done in hell.

These are the things, brethren beloved, which we have seen,
and do testify being adjured of you, as he beareth witness who
died for us and rose again. For like as it is written, so was it
performed in every point.

But when the paper was wholly read through, all that heard
it fell upon their faces weeping bitterly and smote hard upon
their breasts, crying out and saying: "Woe unto us: wherefore
cometh this to pass unto us wretched men?" Pilate did flee, Annas
and Caiaphas did flee, the priests and Levites did flee, and all
the people of the Jews beside, lamenting and saying: "Woe unto
us miserable men; we have shed innocent blood upon the earth."

Therefore for three days and three nights they tasted not at
all either bread or water, neither did any of them return unto
the synagogue.[6]

". . . ON THE THIRD DAY HE AROSE AGAIN FROM THE DEAD AND ASCENDED INTO HEAVEN . . ."

*As early as the second century a Gospel of Peter was known to
have existed, for Serapion, Bishop of Antioch from 199 to 211,
wrote to the church of Rhossus withdrawing a permission he had
formerly given to read from the work in church on the grounds
that it was Docetic, that is, comforming to a heretical doctrine
which held that the humanity and suffering of Jesus on earth
were illusions. It was not until the winter of 1886–87, however,
that a single quotation from it was known. At this time a fragment
of the ancient manuscript was found in the grave of a Christian
monk of the period between the eighth and the twelfth century.
It is now in the Cairo Museum. Its origin is believed to have
been in Gnostic circles in Syria. The following selection is taken
from it.*

Now in the night whereon the Lord's day dawned, as the
soldiers were keeping guard two by two in every watch, there

came a great sound in the heaven, and they saw the heavens opened and two men descend thence, shining with a great light, and drawing near unto the sepulchre. And that stone which had been set on the door rolled away of itself and went back to the side, and the sepulchre was opened and both of the young men entered in.

When therefore those soldiers saw that, they waked up the centurion and the elders (for they also were there keeping watch); and while they were yet telling them the things which they had seen, they saw again three men come out of the sepulchre, and two of them sustaining the other and a cross following after them. And of the two they saw that their hands reached unto heaven, but of him that was led by them that it overpassed the heavens. And they heard a voice out of the heavens saying: "Hast thou preached unto them that sleep?"

And an answer was heard from the cross, saying: "Yea."

Those men therefore took counsel one with another to go and report these things unto Pilate. And while they yet thought thereabout, again the heavens were opened and a man descended and entered into the tomb. And they that were with the centurion when they saw that, hasted to go by night unto Pilate and left the sepulchre whereon they were keeping watch, and told all that they had seen, and were in great agony, saying: "Of a truth he was the son of God."

Pilate answered and said: "I am clear from the blood of the son of God, but thus it seemed good unto you."

Then all they came and besought him and exhorted him to charge the centurion and the soldiers to tell nothing of that they had seen: "For," they said, "it is expedient for us to incur the greatest sin before God, rather than to fall into the hands of the people of the Jews and to be stoned."

Pilate therefore charged the centurion and the soldiers that they should say nothing.

Now early on the Lord's day Mary Magdalene, a disciple of the Lord—which, being afraid because of the Jews, for they were inflamed with anger, had not performed at the sepulchre of the

Lord those things which women are accustomed to do unto them that die and are beloved of them—took with her the women her friends and came unto the tomb where he was laid. And they feared lest the Jews should see them, and said: "Even if we were not able to weep and lament him on that day whereon he was crucified, yet let us now do so at his tomb. But who will roll away for us the stone also that is set upon the door of the tomb, that we may enter in and sit beside him and perform that which is due? for the stone was great, and we fear lest any man see us. And if we cannot do so, yet let us cast down at the door these things which we bring for a memorial of him, and we will weep and lament until we come unto our house."

And they went and found the sepulchre open: and they drew near and looked in there, and saw there a young man sitting in the midst of the sepulchre, of a fair countenance and clad in very bright raiment, which said unto them: "Wherefore are ye come? whom seek ye? not him that was crucified? He is risen and is departed; but if ye believe it not, look in and see the place where he lay, that he is not *here:* for he is risen and is departed thither whence he was sent."[7]

Again we draw on the Acts of Pilate, which are concerned with many phases of the story of Jesus' death and reported resurrection here to tell of the mysterious disappearance of the body of the crucified one from the tomb in which it had been laid.

And . . . there came certain of the guard which the Jews had asked of Pilate to keep the sepulchre of Jesus lest peradventure his disciples should come and steal him away. And they spake and declared unto the rulers of the synagogue and the priests and the Levites that which had come to pass: how that there was a great earthquake, and we saw an angel descend from heaven, and he rolled away the stone from the mouth of the cave, and sat upon it. And he did shine like snow and like lightning, and we were sore afraid and lay as dead men. And we heard the voice of the angel speaking with the women which waited at the sepulchre, saying: "Fear ye not: for I know that ye seek Jesus which was crucified. He is not here: he is risen, as he said. Come, see the place where the Lord lay, and go quickly and say unto his disciples that he is risen from the dead, and is in Galilee."

The Jews say: "With what women spake he?"

They of the guard say: "We know not who they were."

The Jews say: "At what hour was it?"

They of the guard say: "At midnight."

The Jews say: "And wherefore did ye not take the women?"

They of the guard say: "We were become as dead men through fear, and we looked not to see the light of the day; how then could we take them?"

The Jews say: "As the Lord liveth, we believe you not."

They of the guard say unto the Jews: "So many signs saw ye in that man, and ye believed not, how then should ye believe us? Verily ye sware rightly 'as the Lord liveth,' for he liveth indeed."

Again they of the guard say: "We have heard that ye shut up him that begged the body of Jesus, and that ye sealed the door; and when ye had opened it ye found him not. Give ye therefore Joseph and we will give you Jesus."

The Jews say: "Joseph is departed unto his own city."

They of the guard say unto the Jews: "Jesus also is risen, as we have heard of the angel, and he is in Galilee."

And when the Jews heard these words they were sore afraid, saying: "Take heed lest this report be heard and all men incline unto Jesus."

And the Jews took counsel and laid down much money and gave it to the soldiers, saying: "Say ye: 'While we slept his disciples came by night and stole him away.' And if this come to the governor's hearing we will persuade him and secure you." And they took the money and did as they were instructed.

Now a certain priest named Phinees and Addas a teacher and Aggaeus, a Levite, came down from Galilee unto Jerusalem and told the rulers of the synagogue and the priests and the Levites, saying: "We saw Jesus and his disciples sitting upon the mountain which is called Mamilch, and he said unto his disciples: 'Go into all the world and preach unto every creature: he that believeth and is baptized shall be saved, but he that disbelieveth shall be condemned.'"

And while Jesus yet spake unto his disciples we saw him taken up into heaven.[8]

". . . THENCE HE SHALL COME TO JUDGE THE LIVING AND THE DEAD. . . ."

The original text of The Book of John the Evangelist, that is, the Apostle John, known during the life of Jesus as "the beloved Disciple," was, according to scholarly opinions, a heretical production of the Bogomils, a sect which originated in Bulgaria, and whose influence spread to Thrace and Constantinople. It was finally merged with Islam, and forgotten as an heretical Christian sect. In its original doctrine the book denied that the world was created by God, declaring instead that it was the work of the devil. The Bogomils denied the value of both baptism and the Eucharist. Other heresies brought condemnation upon them by the Church. The following selection, which is on the whole consistent with orthodox Christian doctrine, is believed to have been an insertion into the book, the heretical parts of which have been lost.

I asked the Lord concerning the day of judgement: "What shall be the sign of thy coming?"

And he answered and said unto me: "When the numbers of the righteous shall be accomplished, that is, the number of the righteous that are crowned, then shall Satan be loosed out of his prison, having great wrath, and shall make war with the righteous, and they shall cry unto the Lord with a loud voice. And immediately the Lord shall command an angel to blow with the

trumpet, and the voice of the archangel shall be heard in the
trumpet from heaven even unto hell.

"And then shall the sun be darkened and the moon shall not
give her light, and the stars shall fall, and the four winds shall be
loosed from their foundations, and shall cause the earth and the
sea and the mountains to quake together. And the heaven shall
immediately shake and the sun shall be darkened, and it shall
shine even to the fourth hour. Then shall appear the sign of the
son of man, and all the holy angels with him, and he shall set his
seat upon the clouds, and sit on the throne of his majesty with
the twelve apostles on the twelve seats of their glory. And the
books shall be opened and he shall judge the whole world and
the faith which he proclaimed. And then shall the son of man
send his angels, and they shall gather his elect from the four
winds, from the heights of the heavens unto the boundaries of
them, and shall bring them.

"Then shall the son of God send the evil spirits, to bring all
nations before him, and shall say unto them: 'Come, ye that did
say: "We have eaten and drunk and received the gain of this
world."' And after that they shall again be brought, and shall
all stand before the judgement-seat, even all nations, in fear.
And the books of life shall be opened and all nations shall show
forth their ungodliness. And he shall glorify the righteous for
their patience: and glory and honour and incorruption shall be
the reward of their good works: but as for them that kept the
commandments of the angels and obeyed unrighteously, indignation and trouble and anguish shall take hold on them.

"And the son of God shall bring forth the elect out of the midst
of the sinners and say unto them: 'Come, ye blessed of my
Father, inherit the kingdom prepared for you from the foundation of the world.' Then shall he say unto the sinners: 'Depart
from me, ye cursed, into everlasting fire, which was prepared for
the devil and his angels.' And the rest, beholding the last cutting
off, shall cast the sinners into hell by the commandment of the
invisible Father.

"Then shall the spirits of them that believe not go forth out of the prisons, and then shall my voice be heard, and there shall be one fold and one shepherd: and the darkness and obscurity shall come forth out of the lower parts of the earth—that is to say, the darkness of the gehenna of fire—and shall burn all things from below even to the air of the firmament. And the Lord shall be in the firmament and even to the lower parts of the earth. . . . And then shall Satan and all his host be bound and cast into the lake of fire. And the son of God shall walk with his elect above the firmament and shall shut up the devil, binding him with strong chains that cannot be loosed.

"At that time the sinners, weeping and mourning, shall say: 'O earth, swallow us up and cover us in death.' And then shall the righteous shine as the sun in the kingdom of their Father. And he shall bring them before the throne of the invisible Father, saying: 'Behold, I and my children whom God hath given me: O righteous one, the world hath not known thee, but I have known thee in truth, because thou hast sent me.'

"And then shall the Father answer his son and say: 'My beloved son, sit thou on my right hand until I make thine enemies the footstool of thy feet, which have denied me and said: We are gods, and beside us there is none other god: which have slain thy prophets and persecuted thy righteous ones, and thou hast persecuted them even unto the outer darkness: there shall be weeping and gnashing of teeth.'

"And then shall the son of God sit on the right hand of his Father, and the Father shall command his angels, and they shall minister unto them [i.e., the righteous] and set them among the choirs of the angels, to clothe them with incorruptible garments, and shall give them crowns that fade not and seats that cannot be moved. And God shall be in the midst of them; and they shall not hunger nor thirst any more, neither shall the sun light on them nor any heat. And God shall wipe away every tear from their eyes. And he shall reign with his holy Father, and of his kingdom there shall be no end for ever and ever."[9]

7

---◆---

THE LATER APPEARANCES OF JESUS

TO PETER

The Acts of Peter, from which the first of the following selections is taken, is probably the work of a resident of Asia Minor who lived sometime between A.D. 160 and 200. Portions of it exist in Coptic, Slavonic, Syriac, Armenian, Arabic, Ethiopic, Latin, and Greek.

Now Peter was in Rome rejoicing in the Lord with the brethren, and giving thanks night and day for the multitude which was brought daily unto the holy name by the grace of the Lord. . . .

And whereas there was great trouble in Rome, Albinus made known his state unto Agrippa, saying to him: "Either do thou avenge me of Peter that hath withdrawn my wife, or I will avenge myself."

And Agrippa said: "I have suffered the same at his hand, for he hath withdrawn my concubines."

And Albinus said unto him: "Why then tarriest thou, Agrippa? let us find him and put him to death for a dealer in curious arts, that we may have our wives again, and avenge them also which are not able to put him to death, whose wives also he hath parted from them."

And as they considered these things, Xanthippe took knowledge of the counsel of her husband with Agrippa, and sent and showed Peter, that he might depart from Rome. And the rest of the brethren, together with Marcellus, besought him to depart.

But Peter said unto them: "Shall we be runaways, brethren?"
And they said to him: "Nay, but that thou mayest yet be able
to serve the Lord."

And he obeyed the brethren's voice and went forth alone,
saying: "Let none of you come forth with me, but I will go forth
alone, having changed the fashion of mine apparel."

And as he went forth of the city, he saw the Lord entering
into Rome. And when he saw him, he said: "Lord, whither
goest thou thus?" ["*Quo vadis?*"]

And the Lord said unto him: "I go into Rome to be crucified."

And Peter said unto him: "Lord, art thou being crucified
again?"

He said unto him: "Yea, Peter, I am being crucified again."

And Peter came to himself: and having beheld the Lord as-
cending up into heaven, he returned to Rome, rejoicing, and
glorifying the Lord, for that he said: "I am being crucified":* the
which was about to befall Peter.

He went up therefore again unto the brethren, and told them
that which had been seen by him: and they lamented in soul,
weeping and saying: "We beseech thee, Peter, take thought for
us that are young."

And Peter said unto them: "If it be the Lord's will, it cometh
to pass, even if we will it not; but for you, the Lord is able to
stablish you in his faith, and will found you therein and make you
spread abroad, whom he himself hath planted, that ye also may
plant others through him. But I, so long as the Lord will that I
be in the flesh, resist not; and again if he take me to him I rejoice
and am glad."

And while Peter thus spake, and all the brethren wept, behold four soldiers took him and led him unto Agrippa. And he in
his madness commanded him to be crucified on an accusation of
godlessness. The whole multitude of the brethren therefore ran
together, both of rich and poor, orphans and widows, weak and
strong, desiring to see and to rescue Peter, while the people

* Roman tradition places the spot at which this meeting took place
beside the Appian Way. The "Quo Vadis" church now marks it. —Ed.

shouted with one voice, and would not be silenced: "What wrong hath Peter done, O Agrippa? Wherein hath he hurt thee? Tell the Romans!"

And others said: "We fear lest if this man die, his Lord destroy us all."

And Peter when he came unto the place stilled the people and said: "Ye men that are soldiers of Christ! ye men that hope in Christ! remember the signs and wonders which ye have seen wrought through me, remember the compassion of God, how many cures he hath wrought for you. Wait for him that cometh and shall reward every man according to his doings. And now be ye not bitter against Agrippa; for he is the minister of his father's working. And this cometh to pass at all events, for the Lord hath manifested unto me that which befalleth. But why delay I and draw not near unto the cross?"

And having approached and standing by the cross he began to say: "O name of the cross, thou hidden mystery! O grace ineffable that is pronounced in the name of the cross! O nature of man, that cannot be separated from God! O love unspeakable and inseparable, that cannot be shown forth by unclean lips! I seize thee now, I that am at the end of my delivery hence. I will declare thee, what thou art: I will not keep silence of the mystery of the cross which of old was shut and hidden from my soul. Let not the cross be unto you which hope in Christ, this which appeareth: for it is another thing, different from that which appeareth, even this passion which is according to that of Christ. And now above all, because ye that can hear are able to hear it of me, that am at the last and final hour of my life, hearken: Separate your souls from every thing that is of the senses, from every thing that appeareth, and does not exist in truth. Blind these eyes of yours, close these ears of yours, put away your doings that are seen; and ye shall perceive that which concerneth Christ, and the whole mystery of your salvation: and let thus much be said unto you that hear, as if it had not been spoken.

"But now it is time for thee, Peter, to deliver up thy body unto them that take it. Receive it then, ye unto whom it belongeth. I beseech you the executioners, crucify me thus, with the head downward and not otherwise: and the reason wherefore, I will tell unto them that hear."

And when they had hanged him up after the manner he desired, he began again to say: "Ye men unto whom it belongeth to hear, hearken to that which I shall declare unto you at this especial time as I hang here. . . . For it is right to mount upon the cross of Christ, who is the word stretched out, the one and only, of whom the spirit saith: For what else is Christ, but the word, the sound of God? So that the word is the upright beam whereon I am crucified. And the sound is that which crosseth it, the nature of man. And the nail which holdeth the cross-tree unto the upright in the midst thereof is the conversion and repentance of man." . . .

And when the multitude that stood by pronounced the Amen with a great sound, together with the Amen Peter gave up his spirit unto the Lord.[1]

TO ANDREW AND MATTHIAS (MATTHEW)

Little is known about the origin of The Acts of Andrew and Matthias, from which this account of a post-resurrection appearance of Jesus is taken. It was at one time thought to have been a part of an earlier apocryphal book known as The Acts of Andrew, but since there seems no place in that work for the story told here, scholars have come to the conclusion that the two are quite independent of each other. The date of its composition is unknown.

At that time all the apostles were gathered together and divided the countries among themselves, casting lots. And it fell to Matthias to go to the land of the anthropophagi. Now the men of that city ate no bread nor drank wine, but ate the flesh and drank the blood of men; and every stranger who landed there they took, and put out his eyes, and gave him a magic drink which took away his understanding. So when Matthias arrived he was so treated; but the drink had no effect on him, and he remained praying for help in the prison.

And a light came and a voice: "Matthias, my beloved, receive sight." And he saw. And the voice continued: "I will not forsake thee: abide twenty-seven days, and I will send Andrew to deliver thee and all the rest." And the Saviour went up into heaven.

Matthias remained singing praises; when the executioners came to take victims, he kept his eyes closed. They came and looked at the ticket on his hand and said: "Three days more and we will slay him." For every victim had a ticket tied on his hand to show the date when his thirty days would be fulfilled.

When twenty-seven days had elapsed, the Lord appeared to Andrew in the country where he was teaching and said: "In three days Matthias is to be slain by the man-eaters; go and deliver him."

"How is it possible for me to get there in time?"

"Early to-morrow, go to the shore and you will find a ship." And he left him.

They went, Andrew and his disciples, and found a little boat and three men. The pilot was the Lord, and the other two were angels. Andrew asked whither they were going. "To the land of the man-eaters."

"I would go there too."

"Every man avoids that place; why will you go?"

"I have an errand to do; and if you can, take us."

He said: "Come on board."

Andrew said: "I must tell you we have neither money nor victuals."

"How then do you travel?"

"Our master forbade us to take money and provisions. If you will do us this kindness, tell us: if not, we will look for another ship."

"If these are your orders, come on board and welcome; I desire truly to have disciples of Jesus on my ship." So they embarked.

Jesus ordered three loaves to be brought, and Andrew summoned his disciples to partake; but they could not answer him, for they were disturbed with the sea. So Andrew explained to the pilot, and he offered to set them ashore: but they refused to leave Andrew.

Jesus said: "Tell your disciples some of the wonders your master did, to encourage them, for we are going to set sail." So they did, and Jesus steered.

Jesus seeing that they were near land, leaned his head on an angel and ceased speaking to Andrew: and Andrew went to sleep. Then Jesus bade the angels take the men and lay them outside the city of the man-eaters and return: and then all departed to heaven.

Andrew awoke and looked about him and realized what had happened, and roused his disciples. . . .

Andrew rejoiced and prayed the Lord to show himself: and Jesus appeared in the form of a beautiful young child. Andrew asked pardon for his boldness on the ship. Jesus reassured him and told him what trials awaited him in the city, and encouraged him to endure them, and departed.

They entered the city, unseen, and went to the prison. The seven guards fell dead at his prayer: at the sign of the cross the doors opened. He found Matthias and they greeted each other. Andrew looked at the victims, who were naked and eating grass, and smote his breast and reproached the devil: "How long warrest thou with men? thou didst cause Adam to be cast out of paradise: thou didst cause his bread that was on the table to be turned to stones. Again, thou didst enter into the mind of the angels and cause them to be defiled with women and madest their savage sons the giants to devour men on the earth, so that God sent the flood. . . ."

Then they both prayed, and they laid their hands on the prisoners and restored first their sight and then their sense, and Andrew bade them go out of the city and remain under a fig-tree and await him: there were 270 men and 49 women. And Andrew commanded a cloud, and it took Matthias and the disciples and brethren to the mount where Peter was teaching, and there they remained.[2]

TO THOMAS

The work from which the story of Thomas' sale to Gundaphorus is taken is of considerable length. It was probably originally composed in Greek at an uncertain date and early translated into Syriac. It exists in both languages. Portions of it in Ethiopic and Latin are also known. Gundaphorus was an historical personage who reigned over a part of India in the first century after the birth of Jesus. His coins bear his name in Greek as "Hyndopheres."

At that season all we the apostles were at Jerusalem, Simon which is called Peter and Andrew his brother, James the son of Zebedee and John his brother, Philip and Bartholomew, Thomas and Matthew the publican, James the son of Alphaeus and Simon the Canaanite, and Judas the brother of James: and we divided the regions of the world, that every one of us should go unto the region that fell to him and unto the nation whereunto the Lord sent him.

According to the lot, therefore, India fell unto Judas Thomas, which is also the twin: but he would not go, saying that by reason of the weakness of the flesh he could not travel, and "I am an Hebrew man; how can I go amongst the Indians and preach the truth?"

And as he thus reasoned and spake, the Saviour appeared unto him by night and saith to him: "Fear not, Thomas, go thou unto India and preach the word there, for my grace is with thee."

But he would not obey, saying: "Whither thou wouldest send me, send me, but elsewhere, for unto the Indians I will not go."

And while he thus spake and thought, it chanced that there was there a certain merchant come from India whose name was Abbanes, sent from the King Gundaphorus, and having

commandment from him to buy a carpenter and bring him unto
him.

Now the Lord seeing him walking in the market-place at
noon said unto him: "Wouldest thou buy a carpenter?"

And he said to him: "Yea."

And the Lord said to him: "I have a slave that is a carpenter
and I desire to sell him." And so saying he showed him Thomas
afar off, and agreed with him for three litrae of silver unstamped,
and wrote a deed of sale, saying: "I, Jesus, the son of Joseph
the carpenter, acknowledge that I have sold my slave, Judas
by name, unto thee Abbanes, a merchant of Gundaphorus, king
of the Indians."

And when the deed was finished, the Saviour took Judas
Thomas and led him away to Abbanes the merchant; and when
Abbanes saw him he said unto him: "Is this thy master?"

And the apostle said: "Yea, he is my Lord."

And he said: "I have bought thee of him." And the apostle
held his peace.

And on the day following the apostle arose early, and having
prayed and besought the Lord he said: "I will go whither thou
wilt, Lord Jesus: thy will be done." And he departed unto
Abbanes the merchant, taking with him nothing at all save
only his price. For the Lord had given it unto him, saying:
"Let thy price also be with thee, together with my grace,
wheresoever thou goest."[3]

TO THE TWELVE APOSTLES

*The following fragment is believed to be Fragment II of The
Gospel of Peter. It obviously purports to be an account of a
meeting between Jesus and the apostles that occurred after the
resurrection and the ascent into heaven, described elsewhere,
though this is not specifically stated. It begins abruptly with a
discourse by Jesus.*

Many of them shall be false prophets, and shall teach ways
and diverse doctrines of perdition. And they shall become sons

of perdition. And then shall God come unto my faithful ones that hunger and thirst and are afflicted and prove their souls in this life, and shall judge the sons of iniquity.

And the Lord added and said: "Let us go unto the mountain (and) pray."

And going with him, we the twelve disciples besought him that he would show us one of our righteous brethren that had departed out of the world, that we might see what manner of men they are in their form, and take courage, and encourage also the men that should hear us. And as we prayed, suddenly there appeared two men standing before the Lord upon whom we were not able to look. For there issued from their countenance a ray as of the sun, and their raiment was shining so as the eye of man never saw the like: for no mouth is able to declare nor heart to conceive the glory wherewith they were clad and the beauty of their countenance. Whom when we saw we were astonished, for their bodies were whiter than any snow and redder than any rose. And the redness of them was mingled with the whiteness, and, in a word, I am not able to declare their beauty. For their hair was curling and flourishing [flowery], and fell comely about their countenance and their shoulders like a garland woven of nard and various flowers, or like a rainbow in the air: such was their comeliness.

We, then, seeing the beauty of them were astonished at them, for they appeared suddenly. And I drew near to the Lord and said: "Who are these?"

He saith to me: "These are your righteous brethren whose appearance ye did desire to see."

And I said unto him: "And where are all the righteous? or of what sort is the world wherein they are, and possess this glory?"

And the Lord showed me a very great region outside this world exceeding bright with light, and the air of that place illuminated with the beams of the sun, and the earth of itself flowering with blossoms that fade not, and full of spices and plants, fair-flowering and incorruptible, and bearing blessed fruit. And so great was the blossom that the odour thereof was borne thence even unto us.

And the dwellers in that place were clad with the raiment of shining angels, and their raiment was like unto their land. And angels ran round about them there. And the glory of them that dwelt there was all equal, and with one voice they praised the Lord God, rejoicing in that place.

The Lord saith unto us: "This is the place of your leaders, the righteous men."

And I saw also another place over against that one, very squalid; and it was a place of punishment, and they that were punished and the angels that punished them had their raiment dark, according to the air of the place. And some there were there hanging by their tongues; and these were they that blasphemed the way of righteousness, and under them was laid fire flaming and tormenting them. And there was a great lake full of flaming mire, wherein were certain men that turned away from righteousness; and angels, tormentors, were set over them.

And there were also others, women, hanged by their hair above that mire which boiled up; and these were they that adorned themselves for adultery. And the men that were joined with them in the defilement of adultery were hanging by their feet, and had their heads hidden in the mire, and said: "We believed not that we should come unto this place."

And I saw the murderers and them that were consenting to them cast into a strait place full of evil, creeping things, and smitten by those beasts, and so turning themselves about in that torment. And upon them were set worms like clouds of darkness. And the souls of them that were murdered stood and looked upon the torment of those murderers and said: "O God, righteous is thy judgement."

And hard by that place I saw another strait place wherein the discharge and the stench of them that were in torment ran down, and there was as it were a lake there. And there sat women up to their necks in that liquor, and over against them many children which were born out of due time sat crying: and from them went forth rays of fire and smote the women in the eyes: and these were they that conceived out of wedlock and caused abortion.

And other men and women were being burned up to their middle and cast down in a dark place and scourged by evil spirits, and having their entrails devoured by worms that rested not. And these were they that had persecuted the righteous and delivered them up.

And near to them again were women and men gnawing their lips and in torment, and having iron heated in the fire set against their eyes. And these were they that did blaspheme and speak evil of the way of righteousness.

And over against these were yet others, men and women, gnawing their tongues and having flaming fire in their mouths. And these were the false witnesses.

And in another place were gravel-stones sharper than swords or any spit, heated with fire, and men and women clad in filthy rags rolled upon them in torment. And these were they that were rich and trusted in their riches, and had no pity upon orphans and widows but neglected the commandments of God.

And in another great lake full of foul matter and blood and boiling mire stood men and women up to their knees. And these were they that lent money and demanded usury upon usury.

And other men and women being cast down from a great rock fell to the bottom, and again were driven by them that were set over them, to go up upon the rock, and thence were cast down to the bottom and had no rest from this torment. And these were they that did defile their bodies, behaving as women: and the women that were with them were they that lay with one another as a man with a woman.

And beside that rock was a place of much fire, and there stood men which with their own hands had made images for themselves instead of God. And beside them other men and women having rods of fire and smiting one another and never resting from this manner of torment. . . .

And yet others near unto them, men and women, burning

and turning themselves about and roasted as in a pan. And
these were they that forsook the way of God.[4]

TO MARY AT HER ASSUMPTION

*The following account from a little-known work may be the
source of the dogma of the Assumption of Mary, promulgated in
a fairly recent time.*

On the twentieth of the month Tobi, they [the disciples]
were all gathered at the altar, and Jesus appeared and greeted
them. He bade Peter prepare the altar because "I must needs
take a great offering from your midst on the morrow, before that
each one of you goes to the lot that hath fallen to him to preach
therein." He then ordained Peter archbishop, and others, including Evodius, presbyters, and also deacons, readers, psalmists,
and doorkeepers; and departed to heaven. They remained,
wondering what the offering was to be.

On the twenty-first of Tobi, Jesus returned, on the chariot of
the cherubim, with thousands of angels, and David the sweet
singer. We besought him to tell what the great offering was to
be, and he told them that it was his Mother whom he was to
take to himself.

We all wept, and Peter asked if it was not possible that Mary
should never die, and then if she might not be left to them
for a few days. But the Lord said that her time was accomplished. The women, and also Mary, wept, but Jesus con-
soled her.

She said: "I have heard that Death has many terrible faces.
How shall I bear to see them?"

He said: "How dost thou fear his divine shape when the
Life of all the world is with thee?" And he kissed her, and
blessed them all, and bade Peter look upon the altar for heavenly
garments which the Father had sent to shroud Mary in.

Mary arose and was arrayed in the garments, and turned to
the east and uttered a prayer in the language of heaven, and

then lay down, still facing eastward. Jesus made us stand for
the prayer, and the virgins also who used to minister in the
temple and had come to wait on Mary after the Passion.

We asked them why they left it. They said: "When we saw
the darkness at the crucifixion we fled into the holy of holies
and shut the door. We saw a strong angel come down with a
sword, and he rent the veil in twain: and we heard a great
voice saying, 'Woe to thee, Jerusalem, which killest the prophets.'
The angel of the altar flew up into the canopy of the altar
with the angel of the sword: and we knew that God had left
his people, and we fled to his Mother."

The virgins stood about Mary singing, and Jesus sat by her.
She besought him to save her from the many terrors of the next
world—the accusers of Amenti, the dragon of the abyss, the
river of fire that proves the righteous and the wicked.

He comforted her and said to the apostles: "Let us withdraw outside for a little while, for Death cannot approach while
I am here." And they went out and he sat on a stone, and
looked up to heaven and groaned and said: "I have overcome
thee, O Death, that dwellest in the storehouses of the south.
Come, appear to my virgin mother: but not in a fearful shape."

He appeared, and when she saw him, her soul leaped into
the bosom of her son—white as snow, and he wrapped it in
garments of fine linen and gave it to Michael.

All the women wept; Salome ran to Jesus and said: "Behold,
she whom thou lovest is dead."

David the singer rejoiced and said: "Right dear in the sight of
the Lord is the death of his saints."

They re-entered the house and found her lying dead, and
Jesus blessed her. Jesus shrouded the body in the heavenly
garments, and they were fastened thereto. He bade the apostles
take up the body, Peter bearing the head and John the feet,
and carrying it to a new tomb in the field of Jehoshaphat, and
watch it for three and a half days.

David rejoiced, saying: "She shall be brought unto the king in
raiment of needlework; the virgins, her companions, that follow

her shall be brought unto thee," [Psalm 45:14] and "Arise, O Lord, unto thy rest; thou and the ark of thy strength" [Psalm 132:8].

Jesus ascended with Mary's soul in the chariot of the cherubim. We took up the body, and when we came to the field of Jehoshaphat, the Jews heard the singing and came out intending to burn the body. But a wall of fire encompassed us, and they were blinded: and the body was laid in the tomb and watched for three and a half days.

The Jews were in terror and confessed their sin and asked pardon. Their eyes were opened and they sought and found not the body: and they were amazed and confessed themselves guilty.

At mid-day on the fourth day all were gathered at the tomb. A great voice came, saying: "Go every one to his place till the seventh month: for I have hardened the heart of the Jews, and they will not be able to find the tomb or the body till I take it up to heaven. Return on the 16th of Mesore."

We returned to the house.

In the seventh month after the death, i.e. on 15th of Mesore, we reassembled at the tomb and spent the night in watching and singing. At dawn on the 16th of Mesore, Jesus appeared.

Peter said: "We are grieved that we have not seen thy Mother since her death."

Jesus said: "She shall now come."

The chariot of the cherubim appeared with the Virgin seated in it. There were greetings. Jesus bade the apostles go and preach in all the world. He spent all that day with us and with his Mother, and gave us the salutation of peace and went up to heaven in glory.

Such was the death of the Virgin on the 21st of Tobi, and her assumption on 16th Mesore. I, Evodius, saw it all.[5]

TO A BRIDE AND GROOM

The following episode, a part of the story of Thomas' mission to India, is one of the strange evidences of the obsession against sex that is displayed in many of the apocryphal New Testament writings. The setting is a wedding feast in India for the daughter of a king and her bridegroom.

And the king desired the groomsmen to depart out of the bride-chamber; and when all were gone out and the doors were shut, the bridegroom lifted up the curtain of the bride-chamber to fetch the bride unto him. And he was the Lord Jesus bearing the likeness of Judas Thomas and speaking with the bride—even of him that but now had blessed them and gone out from them, the apostle; and he saith unto him: "Wentest thou not out in the sight of all? How then art thou found here?"

But the Lord said to him: "I am not Judas which is also called Thomas, but I am his brother." And the Lord sat down upon the bed and bade them also sit upon chairs, and said unto them: "Remember, my children, what my brother spake unto you and what he delivered before you. Know this, that if ye abstain from this foul intercourse, ye become holy temples, pure, being quit of impulses and pains, seen and unseen, and ye will acquire no cares of life or of children, whose end is destruction: and if indeed ye get many children, for their sakes ye become grasping and covetous, stripping orphans and overreaching widows, and by so doing subject yourselves to grievous punishments. For the more part of children become useless, oppressed of devils, some openly and some invisibly, for they become either lunatic or half withered or blind or deaf or dumb or paralytic or foolish; and if they be sound, again they will be vain, doing useless or abominable acts; for they will be caught either in adultery or murder or theft or fornication, and by all these will ye be afflicted.

"But if ye be persuaded and keep your souls chaste before God, there will come unto you living children whom these blemishes touch not, and ye shall be without care, leading a tranquil life without grief or anxiety, looking to receive that incorruptible and true marriage, and ye shall be therein groomsmen entering into that bride-chamber which is full of immortality and light."

And when the young people heard these things, they believed the Lord and gave themselves up unto him, and abstained from foul desire and continued so, passing the night in that place. And the Lord departed from before them, saying thus: "The grace of the Lord shall be with you."[6]

8

---◆---

THE BOOKS OF THE GNOSTICS

The obscure and abstruse view of Gnosticism in regard to Jesus is well illustrated by three accounts called the Pistis Sophia, The Book of the Savior, and The Gospel of Truth. They are too long, too rambling, and too obscure to include in their entirety here. There follow outlines of the first two, made by G. R. S. Mead, and a condensation of the third from The Gospel of Thomas.

SUMMARY OF THE PISTIS SOPHIA

One of the principal, and least understandable books of Gnosticism is the Pistis Sophia. Its significance lies in its reflection of the basic philosophy of Gnosticism—that is, that salvation comes through gaining the gnosis, or knowledge. The mystical concept of the Sophia was that of the world-soul, wisdom, or ultimate knowledge of all mysteries. Though because of the close connection between Gnosticism and Christianity one may hear echoes in Gnostic literature of the New Testament more often than of the Old, there is in the concept, and in the Pistis Sophia, a reminder of the eighth and ninth chapters of the book of Proverbs: "Doth not wisdom cry, and understanding put forth her voice? She standeth in the top of high places," etc.

But the Sophia, in Gnostic mythology, had many other names. She was not only wisdom and the world soul. She was also the All-Mother, that is, Mother of all living, the Shining Mother, the

*Power Above, the Holy Spirit, the Left Hand of existence, as
the Christos was the Right Hand—and called by many other
names. There is much that is incomprehensible in the following
greatly condensed summary of the Pistis Sophia, but it will
serve to illustrate the obscurity of Gnostic writings.*

The Pistis Sophia treatise begins by informing us that Jesus,
after rising from the dead, spent eleven years with his disciples,
instructing them. So far, however, he had taught them the
mysteries of the inner world up to a certain point only, apparently up to the outermost realms of the Light-world* only,
and yet even so far with omissions of many points which
they were as yet incapable of understanding. . . .

It came to pass . . . in the twelfth year, that the disciples
were assembled with the Master on the Mount of Olives,
rejoicing that they had, as they thought, received all the fullness. . . . Jesus was sitting apart, when, at sunrise, they beheld
a great light-stream pouring over him, so that he became lost to
view in the ineffable radiance, but its rays were of every kind
and type; and in it the Master soared aloft into heaven, leaving
the disciples in great fear and confusion as they silently gazed
after him. . . .

On the ninth hour of the morrow they saw Jesus descending
in infinite light, more brilliant far than when he had ascended.
. . . The disciples were dismayed and in great fear, but Jesus,
the compassionate and merciful-minded, spake unto them, saying: "Take courage, it is I; be not afraid. . . ."

The Master, now speaking as the glorified Christ, bids them
rejoice, for that now he will tell them all things "from the
beginning of the truth to the end thereof," face to face, without
parable, for that authority has now been given him. . . .

For this cause is it that he hath again been clothed in the
vesture of light, the robe of glory, which he had left with the

---

* In Gnosticism "the Light-world" is one of the "Aeons"—the latter
word referring not to a time span, but to one stage of the many that
eventually made it possible to achieve complete enlightenment.

first mystery, in the lowest spaces of the supernal Light-realm. He hath received it in order that he may speak to human kind and reveal all the mysteries, but first of all to the Twelve. For the Twelve are his order, who he hath chosen from the beginning, before he came into the world. . . .

So too . . . was . . . John the Baptizer with water for the remission of sins; not only so, but the soul of John was the soul of Elias reborn in him. These things had he explained before, when he said: "If ye will receive it, John the Baptist is Elias, who, I said, was for to come"; but they had not understood.

Into Mary, his mother, also he had implanted a power higher than them all, "the body which I bore in the height," and also another power instead of the soul, and so Jesus was born. It was he himself who had watched over the birth of his disciples, so that no soul of the world-rulers should be found in them, but one of a higher nature.

And the master continued in his conversation and said unto them: "Lo, I have put on my vesture, and all power hath been given me by the first mystery. Yet a little while and I will tell you the mystery of the pleroma* and the pleroma of the pleroma; I will conceal nothing from you from this hour. . . . Hearken, I will tell you all things which have befallen me.

"It came to pass, when the sun had risen in the regions of the east, that a great stream of light descended in which was my vesture, the same which I had laid up in the four-and-twentieth mystery, as I have said unto you. And I found a mystery in my vesture, written in these five words which pertain to the height: Zama, Zama, Ozza, Rachama, Ozai. And this is the interpretation thereof:

"The mystery which is beyond the world, that whereby all things exist: It is all evolution and all involution; It projected all emanations and all things therein. Because of It all mysteries exist and all their regions."

Hereupon the master recites the hymn of praise and welcome

* Literally, "the fullness," at least in the interpretation of some scholars. —Ed.

sung by the powers at his investiture on the great day "Come unto us"—the day of this supreme initiation, when all his limbs are gathered together. "Come unto us, for we are thy fellow-members (or limbs). We are all one with thee. We are one and the same, and thou art one and the same. This is the first mystery, who hath existed from the beginning in the ineffable,* before he came forth; and the name thereof is all of us. Now, therefore, we all love together for thee at the last limit, which also is the mystery of the interior. That also is part of us. . . .

The hymn proceeds: . . . "Lo, then, the time is fulfilled. Come, therefore, to us quickly, in order that we may clothe thee, until thou hast accomplished the full ministry of the perfections of the first mystery, the ministry appointed for thee by the Ineffable. Come, therefore, to us quickly, in order that we may clothe thee, according to the commandment of the first mystery; for yet a little while, a very little while, and thou shalt come to us, and shalt leave the world. Come, therefore, quickly, that thou mayest receive the whole glory, the glory of the first mystery."

Thereupon, on hearing the hymn of the powers, the master said, he donned the lowest robe of glory, and, changed into pure light, soared upwards and came to the lower firmament. And all the powers of that firmament were in great confusion because of the transcendent light; and on seeing the mystery of their names or powers inscribed in it, leaving their ranks, they bowed down and worshipped, saying: "How hath the Lord of the pleroma changed us without our knowing!" And they all sang together . . . a hymn of praise in harmony.

And so he passed upwards and inwards to the first sphere above the firmament, shining with a radiance forty-and-nine times as great as before, and the gates were opened and he

* Here, as often in Gnostic terminology, one can only guess at the meaning of a word by its use in the context. It is probably a fair assumption to conclude that "the ineffable" refers to the nameless divine creative force of the universe. In this meaning the statement, then, is similar to the Hindu and Taoist concept, and that in Luke 17:21 of the King James Version of the Bible, that divinity dwells in all of us. —Ed.

entered the mansions of the sphere, and the powers were changed and worshipped, and sang hymns of rejoicing as before.

Thence upward and inward he passed to the second sphere, shining with a light nine-and-forty times still more intensified, and the powers of that sphere did as them beneath them, and bowed and worshipped and sang hymns to the interior of the interiors.

Still continuing his triumphal flight, he soared still higher within, to the space of the twelve aeons, shining with radiance forty-and-nine times still further increased. And all the orders and rulers of the aeonic* space were amazed. Those of them called the tyrants, under their great leader Adamas, in ignorance fought against the light; but in vain, for they only expended their strength one against the other, and fell down and became "as the inhabitants of the earth who are dead and who have no breath in them"—that is to say, deprived of the light-spark, like the unknowing among men. . . .

Hereupon, the master having invited questions and interpretations of the mysteries he has revealed, Mary Magdalene, who is throughout represented as the most spiritual by far of all the disciples, comes forward, and being granted permission to speak, interprets a passage from Isaiah by the light of the new teaching. The passage begins with the words: "Where, then, O Egypt, where are thy diviners and ordainers of the hour?"**—and among other things Egypt is said to mean the "inefficacious matter. . . ."

In reply to a question by Philip, it is explained that a conversion of the spheres has been effected to aid the salvation of souls; otherwise the number of perfected souls would have been kept back from its accomplishment, that is to say, of those who shall be counted in the heritage of the height, by means of the

---

* Here is an example of the use of the word "aeon" (here in its adjectival form) to mean a region of space, to which the enlightened may attain, rather than a time span. —Ed.

** This is apparently either an error, or (which is less likely) a citation from an ancient manuscript of Isaiah that has since been lost, for the quotation does not occur in Isaiah as we know it in contemporary translation. —Ed.

mysteries, and shall dwell in the light-treasure. The power of
the rulers is in the matter of the world which they make into
souls. By the victory of the master a third of this power has
been taken from them, and converted to a higher substance.

In answer to Mary's further questioning, it is further explained how this third part of their power was taken away. It
always had been that their power, as it became purified, was
gathered back to the higher world by Melchisedec,* the great
receiver or collector of light, it being continually liberated by
the spheres being made to turn more rapidly, that is to say by
the quickening of evolution owing to the influx of light. The
substance of the rulers is graphically described as "the breath
of their mouths, the tears of their eyes, and the sweat of their
bodies"—the matter out of which souls are made.

But as their power was gradually taken from them, their
kingdom began to be dissolved; the rulers therefore began to
devour their own matter, so that it should not be made into
souls of men and so be purified, and in every way strove to
delay the completion of the number of perfect souls—the crown
of evolution. So it came to pass that they fought against the
great soul of the master as he passed through them, and so he
changed them and their configurations and influences, "and
from that hour they have not had the power to turn towards
the purgation of their matter to devour it."

"I took away a third part of their power; I changed their
revolution; I shortened their circles, and caused their path to
be lightened, and they were greatly hurried, and were thrown
into confusion in their path; and from that hour they have no
more had the power of devouring the matter of the purgation
of the brilliancy of their light."

Thus had he shortened their times and hastened evolution.
"For this cause I said unto you before, 'I have shortened the
times because of my elect.'" The "elect" (Pneumatics) are the
perfect number of souls who shall receive the mysteries; indeed
had not the times been shortened, "there would not have been

* See Psalm 110:4. —Ed.

a single material soul saved, but they would have perished in the fire which is in the flesh of the rulers."*

After these explanations the master continues the narrative of his heaven-journey. All the great powers of the aeonic spaces, when they saw what had happened to their tyrants, adored and sang hymns to the interior of the interiors. And so he passed inward to the veils of the thirteenth aeon. Here, outside this space, He found Pistis Sophia,** sitting alone, mourning and grieving because she had not been brought into the thirteenth aeon, her proper region in the height. She was grieving because of the sufferings brought upon her by Arrogant, one of the three triple powers. But when she saw the radiant light-vesture the master, containing the whole glory of her mystery, the mystery of the thirteenth aeon, she began to sing a song to the light which is in the height, which she had seen in the veil of the treasure of light. And as she sang, the veils of the thirteenth aeon were drawn apart, and her syzygy,*** and her two-and-twenty fellow-emanations within the aeon, making together four-and-twenty emanations who came forth from the great invisible forefather and the two other great triple powers of that space, gazed upon the light of his vesture.

Hereupon follows the mystic story of the sufferings of Pistis Sophia. In the beginning she was in the thirteenth aeon with her companion aeons. By order of the first mystery, she gazed into the height and saw the light of the veil of the treasure of light, and desired to ascend into that glorious realm, but could not. She ceased to do the mystery of the thirteenth aeon and ever sang hymns to the light she had seen.

Hereupon the rulers in the twelve aeons below hated her, because she had ceased to do their mystery—the mystery of

* One is reminded of the much later sect called Calvinists, who believed that only a predestined "elect" could ever enter heaven. All others were condemned to "outer darkness." —Ed.
** Here the term Pistis Sophia probably means "the world soul." —Ed.
*** That is, her double, a concept that existed in one form or another in several ancient religions—notably in that of early Egypt, and actually the Christian concept of body and soul is related. —Ed.

intercourse or sexual union—and desired to go into the height and be above them all.

And Arrogant, the disobedient one, that one of the three triple powers of the thirteenth aeon who refused to give the purity of his light for the benefit of others, but desired to keep it for himself and so be ruler of the thirteenth aeon, led the on-slaught against her. Arrogant is apparently the conservative power of the "matter" of this space. He joined himself to the number of the twelve aeons and fought against the Sophia. He sent forth a great power from his light and other powers from his matter, the reflections of the powers and emanations above, into chaos; and caused the Sophia to look down into the lower regions, that she might see this power and imagine it was the real light to which she aspired. And so in ignorance she descended into matter, saying: "I will go into that region, without my consort, to take the light, which the aeons of light have produced for me, so that I may go to the light of lights, which is in the height of heights."

Thus pondering she went forth from the thirteenth aeon and descended into the twelve; but they pursued her, and so she gradually descended to the regions of chaos, and drew nigh to the light-power which Arrogant had sent below, to devour it. But all the material emanations of Arrogant surrounded her, and the light-power of Arrogant set to work to devour all the light-powers in the Sophia; "it expelled her light and swallowed it, and as for her matter they cast it into chaos. . . ."

And so Sophia was greatly weakened and beset and "cried out exceedingly, she cried on high to that Light of lights which she had seen in the beginning, in which she had trusted [hence is she called Pistis (Faith) Sophia], and began to sing songs of repentance," whereby she might be converted or taken back to the light.

The lengthy incident of the Pistis Sophia occupies pp. 42–181 of the Coptic translation, and her thirteen repentances and songs of praise are a mystical interpretation of a number of

the Psalms of the Second Temple collection and of five of the
Odes of Solomon.

To attain to the knowledge of the light, the human soul (as
the world-soul before it) has to descend into matter. Hence
the Sophia, desiring the light, descends toward its reflection,
from the thirteenth aeon, through the twelve, into the depths
of chaos or unorder, where she seems in danger of entirely
losing all her own innate light or spirit, being continually
deprived of it by the powers of matter. Having descended to
the lowest depths of chaos, she at length reaches the limit,
and the path of her pilgrimage begins to lead upward to
spirit again. . . .

The Sophia first utters seven repentances. At the fourth of
these, the turning point of some sub-cycle of her pilgrimage,
she prays that the image of the light may not be turned from
her, for the time is come when "those who turn in the lowest
regions" should be regarded—"the mystery which is made the
type of the race."

At the sixth the light remits her transgression; viz., that she
quitted her own region and fell into chaos. This perhaps refers
to the dawning of the consciousness of the higher ego in the
lower personality. But as yet the command has not come from
the first mystery to free her entirely from chaos. This may refer
to the higher illumination when the consciousness of the true
spiritual soul is obtained.

Therefore at the conclusion of her seventh repentance, where
she pleads that she has done it all in ignorance, through her
love for the light, Jesus, her syzygy (without the first mystery)
raises her up to a slightly less confined region in chaos, but
Sophia still knows not by whom it is done.

It is only at the ninth stage that the first mystery partly
accepts her repentance and sends Jesus in the form of the
Light to her help, so that she recognizes it. . . .

After the thirteenth repentance, Jesus again, of himself, without the first mystery, emanated a brilliant power of light from
himself, and sent it to aid Sophia, to raise her still higher in

chaos, until the command should come to free her entirely. There
are, therefore, as it seems, three degrees of purification from
the chaotic elements of the lower nature.

Next follows a description of the light-powers, which are to
be closely compared with the description of the three vestures
of glory in the opening pages of the Codex.

Then, while Sophia pours forth hymns of joy, the power
becomes a "crown to her head," and her material propensities
begin to be entirely purified, while the spiritual light-powers
which she has succeeded in retaining during her long combat,
join themselves with the new vesture of light which has descended upon her. . . .

When all this is accomplished the Sophia is completely
purified, and her light-powers are re-established and filled with
new light, by their own co-partner of light, that syzygy without
whom Sophia in the beginning had thought to reach the light
of lights, unaided, and so fell into error.

But all is not yet over; the final victory is not yet won. For
the higher she rises the stronger are the powers or projections
sent against her; they proceed to change their shapes, so that
she now has to struggle against still greater foes, which are
emanated and directed by the subtlest powers of cosmos.

Thereupon Sophia is not only crowned but entirely surrounded
with the light-stream, and further supported on either hand
by Michael and Gabriel, the "sun" and "moon." The "wings of
the great bird" flutter, and the "winged globe" unfolds its pin-
ions, preparatory to its flight. Thus the last great battle begins.

The first mystery looking without directs her attack against
the "cruel crafty powers, passions incarnate," and makes the
Sophia tread underfoot the basilisk with seven heads . . . "so
that no seed can arise from it henceforth," and casting down the
rest of the opposing host.

Thereupon Sophia sings triumphant hymns of praise on being
set free from the bonds of chaos. Thus is she set free and
remembers.

Still the great self-willed one and Adamas, the tyrant, are not yet entirely subdued, for the command has not yet come from the first mystery looking within. Therefore does the first mystery looking without seal their regions and those of their rulers "until three times are accomplished," presumably until the end of the seven cycles or ages, of which the present is said to be the fourth, when the perfect number of those of humanity who reach perfection will pass into the interplanetary *Nirvāna*—to use a Buddhist term. This *Nirvāna*, however, is a state out of time and space, as we know them, and therefore can be reached now and within by very holy men who can attain the highest degree of spiritual contemplation. Then shall the gates of the treasure of the great light be opened and the heights be crossed by the pilgrim.

In the course of the many interpretations of scripture given by the disciples and women disciples, Mary, the Mother of Jesus ("my mother according to matter, thou in whom I dwelt"), who is also one of the women disciples, receives permission to speak and tells a quaint story of the Infancy, otherwise entirely unknown.

And Mary answered and said: "My master, concerning the word which thy power prophesied through David, to wit, 'Mercy and truth are met together, righteousness and peace have kissed each other; truth hath flourished on the earth, and righteousness hath looked down from heaven'—thy power prophesied this word of old concerning thee.

"When thou wert a child, before the Spirit had descended upon thee, when thou wert in the vineyard with Joseph, the Spirit came down from the height, and came unto me in the house, like unto thee, and I knew Him not, but thought that He was thou. And he said unto me, 'Where is Jesus, my Brother, that I may go to meet Him?' And when he had said this unto me I was in doubt, and thought it was a phantom tempting me. I seized him and bound him to the foot of the bed which was in my house, until I had gone to find you in the field—thee and Joseph, and I found you in the vineyard; Joseph was putting up the vine poles.

"It came to pass, therefore, when thou didst hear me saying this thing unto Joseph, that thou didst understand, and thou wert joyful and saidest, 'Where is he, that I may see him? Nay [rather] I am expecting him in this place.' And it came to pass, when Joseph heard thee say these words, that he was disturbed.

"We went together, we entered into the house, we found the Spirit bound to the bed, and we gazed upon thee and him, and found that thou wert like unto him. And he that was bound to the bed was unloosed; he embraced thee and kissed thee, and thou also didst kiss him; ye became one and the same being."

At the end of the story of the Sophia, Mary asks: "My master and saviour, how are the four-and-twenty invisibles [the co-powers of Sophia]; of what type, of what quality; or of what quality is their light?"

And Jesus answered and said unto Mary: "What is there in this world which is comparable to them; or what region in this world is like unto them? Now, therefore, to what shall I liken them; or what shall I say concerning them? For there is nothing in this world with which I can compare them; nor is there a single form to which I can liken them. Indeed, there is nothing in this world which is of the quality of heaven. But, Amen, I say unto you, every one of the invisibles is nine times greater than the heaven [the lower firmament], and the sphere above it, and the twelve aeons all together, as I have already told you on another occasion.

"[Again] there is no light in this world which is superior to that of the sun. Amen, Amen, I say unto you, the four-and-twenty invisibles are more radiant than the light of the sun which is in this world, ten thousand times, as I have told you before on another occasion; but the light of the sun *in its true form*, which is in the space of the virgin of light, is more radiant than the four-and-twenty . . . ten thousand times more radiant."

The master promises further, when he takes them through the various spaces of the unseen world, to bring them all finally into the Twin Spaces of the First Mystery, as far as the supreme Space of the Ineffable, "and ye shall see all their configurations as they really are, without similitude.

"When I bring you into the region of the rulers of the fate-sphere, ye shall see the glory in which they are, and compared with their greatly superior glory, ye will regard this world as the darkness of darkness; and when ye gaze down on the whole world of men, it will be as a speck of dust for you, because of the enormous distance by which [the fate-sphere] will be distant from it, and because of the enormous superiority of its quality over it."

And so shall it be in ever increasing glory of light with each higher space, the lower appearing as a speck of dust from its sublimity, as they are taken through the Twelve Aeons, the Thirteenth Aeon (or the Left), the Midst, the Right (sc., of the cosmic cross), the Light-world, and the Inheritance of Light within it.

Then Mary asks: "Master, will the men of this world who have received the mysteries of light be higher in thy kingdom than the emanations of the Treasure of Light?"

And in answer the master explains the ordering and nature and functions of these great emanations, and how that, at the final time of the completion of the aeon and the ascension of the pleroma, these all shall have a higher place in his kingdom; but this time has not yet come. But high above all of them the souls of men who have received the mysteries of light, shall take precedence.

And Mary said: "Master, my indweller of light hath ears, and I comprehend every word which thou speakest. Now, therefore, O master, concerning the word which thou hast spoken, to wit, 'All the souls of human kind which shall receive the mysteries of light, shall in the inheritance of light take precedence of all the rulers who shall repent, and all them of the region of those who are on the right, and the whole space of the treasure of light'; concerning this word, my master, Thou hast said unto us aforetime, 'The first shall be last and the last shall be first,' that is, the 'last' are the whole race of men who shall be first in the light-kingdom; so also they that are [now] in the space of the space of the height are the 'first.'"

The master then continues in his conversation and tells them of the glorious beings and spaces, of which he will treat in detail in his further teaching, up to the inner space of the first mystery, but of those within these supernal spaces he will not treat in the physical consciousness, for "there is no possibility of speaking of them in this world"; nay, "there is neither quality nor light which resembleth them, not only in this world, but also no comparison in those of the Height of Righteousness." He, however, in lofty language describes the greatness of the five great supporters of the outer space of the first mystery, above or within which is the inner space of the first mystery, and above all the space of the ineffable. . . .

"But he who shall have received the complete mystery of the first mystery of the ineffable, that is to say, the twelve mysteries of the first mystery, one after another . . . shall have the power of exploring all the orders of the inheritance of light, of exploring from without within, from within without, from above below, and from below above, from the height to the depth, and from the depth to the height, from the length to the breadth, and from the breadth to the length; in a word, he shall have the power of exploring all the regions of the inheritances of light, and he shall have the power of remaining in the region which he shall choose in the inheritance of the light-kingdom. . . ."

Hereupon follows a magnificent recital of the perfect Gnosis of such a one, for:

"That mystery knoweth why there is darkness, and why light."

And so on, in great phrases describing the wisdom of the supreme mystery, who knows the reason of the existence of all things: darkness of darkness and light of light; chaos and the treasure of light; judgment and inheritance of light; punishment of sinners and rest of the righteous; sin and baptisms; fire of punishment and seals of light; blasphemies and songs to the

THE BOOKS OF THE GNOSTICS

light; and so on through many pairs of opposites, ending with death and life.

But the recital of the greatness of the supreme Gnosis is not yet ended, for the master continues: "Hearken, therefore, now further, O my disciples, while I tell you the whole Gnosis of the mystery of the ineffable."

It is the Gnosis of pitilessness and compassion; of destruction and everlasting increase; of beasts and creeping things, and metals, seas, and earth, clouds and rain, and so on working downwards from man into nature and upwards through all the supernal realms.

But the disciples are amazed at the glories of the Gnosis of this greatest mystery and lose courage. And Mary said: "O master, if the Gnosis of all these things is in that mystery, who is the man in this world who shall be able to understand that mystery and all its Gnoses, and the manner of all the words which thou hast spoken concerning it?"

And the master said: "Grieve not, my disciples, concerning the mystery of that ineffable, thinking that ye will not understand it. Amen, I say unto you, that mystery is yours, and every one's who shall give ear unto you, and shall renounce the whole world, and all the matter therein, who shall renounce all the evil thoughts that are therein, and shall renounce all the cares of this aeon.

"Now, therefore, will I tell you: Whosoever shall renounce the whole world and all therein, and shall submit himself to the divinity, to him that mystery shall be far more easy than all the mysteries of the kingdom of light; it is far simpler to understand than all the rest, and it is far clearer than them all. He who shall come to a knowledge of that mystery, hath renounced the whole of this world and all its cares. For this cause have I said unto you aforetime: 'Come unto me all ye that are oppressed with cares and labour under their weight, and I will give you rest, for my burden is light and my yoke easy.'"*

* Paraphrase of Matthew 11:28–30.

Let them not be dismayed at the vast complexity of the emanation of the pleroma and the world-process, "for the emanation of the pleroma is its Gnosis." Let but the Christ be born in their hearts by their forsaking the delights of the world, and they shall grow into the being of the pleroma and so possess all its Gnosis.

The master then continues his description of the Gnosis of the mystery of the ineffable, resuming it at the point where he had broken off, and leading them higher and higher into the supernal heights through space after space, and hierarchy after hierarchy, of stupendous being and its emanation, up to the mystery itself, the first mystery who knoweth why he came forth from the last limb of the ineffable. . . .

"The mystery of the ineffable is the one and only word, but there is another [Word] on the tongue of the ineffable; it is the rule of the interpretation of all the words which I have spoken unto you."

It is then explained how that he who receives this one and only word, when he comes forth from the body of the matter of the rulers, becomes a great light-stream, and soars into the height; he stands in no need of apology or symbol, for all powers bow down before the vesture of light in which he is clothed, and sing hymns of praise, and so he passes upwards and onwards, through all the inheritances of light, and higher still until he becometh one with the limbs of the ineffable. "Amen, I say unto you, he shall be in all the regions during the time a man can shoot an arrow."

Hereupon follows a recital of the greatness of such a soul. Beginning with the words, "Though he be a man in the world, yet is he higher than all angels, and shall far surpass them all," it recites in the same form all the grades of the supernal hierarchies of beings from angels upwards, and ends as follows:

"Though he be a man in the world, yet is he higher than the whole region of the Treasure, and shall be exalted above the whole of it.

"Though he be a man in the world, yet shall he be king with

me in my kingdom. He is a man in the world but a king in the light.

"Though he be a man in the world, yet is he a man who is not of the world.

"Amen, I say unto you, that man is myself, and I am that man."

And at the great consummation all such men "shall be fellow-kings with me, they shall sit on my right hand and on my left in my kingdom.

"Amen, I say unto you, these men are myself, and I am these men."

There then follows apparently an interpolation consisting of a quotation from some now unknown Gospel: "Wherefore have I said unto you aforetime, 'In the place where I shall be, there also will be my twelve ministers, but Mary Magdalene and John the virgin shall be higher than all the disciples.'

"And all men who shall receive the mystery in that ineffable shall be on my left hand and on my right, and I am they and they are myself.

"They shall be your equals in all things, and yet your thrones shall be more excellent than theirs, and my throne shall be more excellent than yours and [than those of] all men who shall have found the word of that ineffable."

And Mary thinks that this must be the end of all things and the Gnosis of all gnoses, and so protests: "Master, surely there is no other word of the mystery of that ineffable, nor any other word of the whole Gnosis?"

The Saviour answered and said: "Yea, verily; there is another mystery of the ineffable and another word of the whole Gnosis." Nay, a multitude of words, he might have added.

Then Mary asks whether those who do not receive the mystery of the ineffable before they die, will enter the light-kingdom. The master answers that every one who receives a mystery of light, any one of them, shall after death find rest in the light-world appropriate to his mystery, but no one who has not become a Christ will know the Gnosis of the whole pleroma, for "in all openness I am the Gnosis of the whole pleroma."

So he who receives the First Mystery of the First Mystery shall be king over the spaces of the first saviour in the light-realm, and so on up to the twelfth.

And Mary asks: "Master, how is it that the First Mystery hath twelve mysteries, whereas the ineffable hath but one mystery?"

The answer is that they are really one mystery; this mystery is ordered into twelve, and also into five, and again into three, while still remaining one; they are all different aspects or types of the same mystery.*

The two higher mysteries of the three not only ensure the possessor of them, when he leaves the body, his appropriate lot in the inheritance, but they further bestow boons with regard to others. If a man "perform them in all their configurations, that is to say when he shall have created those mysteries for himself," they give the power of further enabling him to protect one who is not a participator in the words of truth, after his death, so that he shall not be punished. Of course such a man cannot "be brought into the light until he have performed the whole polity of the light of those mysteries, that is to say, the strict renunciation of the world"; but he will be sent back again into "a righteous body, which shall find the God of truth and the higher mysteries. . . ."

Hereupon Andrew is in great amazement, and cannot believe that men of the world like themselves can have so high a destiny reserved for them, and can reach such lofty heights. "This matter, then, is hard for me," he says.

When Andrew had said these words, the spirit of the Saviour was moved in him, and he cried out and said: "How long shall I bear with you, how long shall I suffer you? Do ye still not know and are ye ignorant? Know ye not and do ye not understand that ye are all angels, all archangels, gods and lords, all rulers, all the great invisibles, all those of the midst, those of every region

---

* One is reminded here of the Brihadaranyaka Upanishad of Hinduism, in which it is stated that the many names of gods in Hinduism are only the names of the various powers of the one God—Brahma.

of them that are on the right, all the Great Ones of the emanations of the Light with all their glory; that ye are all, of yourselves and in yourselves in turn, from one mass and one matter,
and one substance; ye are all from the same mixture. . . .

"For this cause, therefore, preach ye to the whole human race,
saying, 'Cease not to seek day and night, until ye have found the
purifying mysteries'; and say unto them, 'Renounce the whole
world, and all the matter therein,' for he who buyeth and selleth
in this world, he who eateth and drinketh of his own matter, who
liveth in his own cares and all his own associations, amasses
ever fresh matter from his matter, in that the whole world, and
all that is therein, and all its associations, are exceedingly material purgations, and they shall make enquiry of every one according to his purity."

This is followed by a long instruction on the nature of the
preaching of the disciples to the world when the master shall
have gone unto the light.

"Say unto them, 'Renounce the whole world and the matter
that is in it, all its cares, all its sins, in a word, all the associations
that are in it, that ye may be worthy of the mysteries of light,
and be saved from all the torments which are in the judgments.'"

They are to renounce mourning, superstition, spells, calumny,
false witness, boasting and pride, gluttony, garrulity, evil ca-
resses, desire of avarice, the love of the world, robbery, evil
words, wickedness, pitilessness, wrath, reviling, pillage, slander-
ing, quarreling, ignorance, villainy, sloth, adultery, murder, hard-
ness of heart and impiety, atheism, magic potions, blasphemy,
doctrines of error—that they may escape the torments of fire
and ice and other graphic horrors of an elaborate hell, capped by
the torments of the Great Dragon of the inexorable Outer Darkness, reserved for the greatest of sins, where such absolutely
unrepentant souls "shall be without existence until the end" of
the aeon; they shall be "frozen up" in the state.

Thus far for the negative side, the things to be abandoned; but for the positive, the things to be done, they are to: "Say unto the men of the world, 'Be ye diligent, that ye may receive the mysteries of light, and enter into the height of the kingdom of light.'"

They are to be gentle, peacemakers, merciful, compassionate, to minister unto the poor and sick and afflicted, be loving unto God, and righteous, and live the life of absolute self-renunciation.

"These are all the boundary marks of the paths of them that are worthy of the mysteries of light."

Unto such and such only are the mysteries to be given; the absolute condition is that they make this renunciation and repent.

"It is because of sinners that I have brought these mysteries into the world, for the remission of all the sins which they have committed from the beginning. Wherefore have I said unto you aforetime, 'I came not to call the righteous.'"

The question now arises as to good men who have not received the mysteries, how will it be with them after death?

"A righteous man who is perfect in all righteousness," answers the master, yet who has not received the mysteries of light, on going forth from the body, is taken charge of by the receivers of light—as distinguished from the receivers of wrath. "Three days shall they journey round with that soul in all the creatures of the world," and pass it through all the elements of the judgments, instructing it therein, and then it shall be taken to the virgin of light and sealed with an excellent seal that it may be carried into a righteous body of the aeons, so that it may in its next birth find the signs of the mysteries of light and inherit the kingdom of light for ever.

So with a man who has only sinned twice or thrice, he shall be sent back into the world according to the type of the sins he hath committed; "I will tell you these types when I shall come to explain the emanation of the pleroma in detail.

"But Amen, Amen, I say unto you, even though a righteous man have not committed any sin at all, it is impossible to take him into the Kingdom of Light, because the sign of the Kingdom of the Mysteries is not with him." He must have Gnosis as well as righteousness.

The question next arises as to the sinner who has repented, and received the mysteries, and then has fallen away, and again repented, provided he be not a hypocrite; "Wilt thou or not that we remit his transgressions unto seven times, and give him the mysteries again?"

The Saviour answered and said: "Remit ye his sin not only unto seven times, but Amen, I say unto you, remit ye it unto him many times seven times, and each time give ye him the mysteries from the beginning, the mysteries which are in the first Space from the exterior; perchance ye will win the soul of that brother, so that he may inherit the kingdom of light. . . .

"Amen, I say unto you, he who shall give life unto a single soul, and shall save it, in addition to his own proper light in the kingdom of light, he shall further receive an additional glory for the soul which he shall have saved, so that he who shall save a host of souls, in addition to his own proper glory in the glory, he shall receive a host of additional glories for the souls which he shall have saved."

Nay, they shall not only give the lower mysteries, but the higher mysteries as well, provided always the man sincerely repent and is not a hypocrite; all mysteries up to the three highest mysteries of the first mystery, "for the first mystery is compassionate and merciful-minded."

"But if that man again transgresseth, and is in any kind of sin, ye shall not remit his sin again from that hour, nor any more accept his repentance; let him be for you a stumbling-block and transgressor.

"For Amen, I say unto you, these three mysteries shall witness against his last repentance for him from that hour. Amen, I say unto you, the soul of that man shall have no more probation for the world of the height henceforth from that hour, but it shall dwell in the habitation of the Dragon of the Outer Darkness."

In all of this the disciples have no choice; if they know a man is sincere, and not a hypocrite or merely curious to know what kind of things the rites of the mysteries are, they must give him these mysteries and not withhold them, even if he be one who has never received any of the lower mysteries; for should they hide them from him, they will be subject to a great judgment.

Beyond the giving of these three higher mysteries they have no power, for they have not sufficient knowledge.

But the case of a man who has fallen away after receiving the highest mysteries they can give, is not entirely hopeless; it is, however, in the hands of the First Mystery and the mystery of the ineffable alone.

These alone can accept repentance from such a man, and grant him the remission of his sins, for these mysteries are "compassionate and merciful-minded, and grant remission of sins at any time."

The question is now raised, Supposing they give the mysteries in error to those who are hypocrites and who have deceived them and have afterwards made a mock of the mysteries "mimicking us and making forgeries of our mysteries," what then are they to do?

In this case they are to appeal to the first mystery, saying: "The mystery which we have given unto these impious and iniquitous souls, they have not performed in a manner worthy of thy mystery, but they have [merely] copied [what we did]; give back [therefore] that mystery unto us, and make them for ever strangers to thy kingdom."

In that hour the mysteries such impious souls have received, shall return to them, and such people can receive pardon from no one save only the Mystery of the Ineffable.

In the case of the unbelieving friends and relatives of those who have received the mysteries, the latter may by their prayers and invocations procure a better lot in the after-death state for their relatives and friends, so that they may be sent back into conditions favourable for their receiving the mysteries in another life.

It is then asked whether the mysteries will save the disciples from the pains of martyrdom. "For they are in exceeding great number who persecute us because of thee, and multitudes pursue us because of thy name, so that if we be submitted to the torture, we shall utter the mystery, that we may immediately depart from the body without suffering pain."

The answer is not clear; every one who has accomplished the first (*i.e.*, highest) of the three higher mysteries, in life, when the time comes to leave the body, shall soar into the Kingdom of Life without need of apology or sign. But it is not said that the pains of martyrdom can be avoided.

But they will be able to help others, for "not only ye, but all men who shall achieve the mystery of the resurrection of the dead, which healeth from demonian possessions, and sufferings, and every disease, [which also healeth] the blind, the lame, the halt, the dumb, and the deaf, [the mystery] which I gave unto you aforetime—whosoever shall receive of these mysteries and achieve them, if he ask for any thing whatever hereafter, poverty or riches, weakness or strength, disease or health, or the whole healing of the body, and the resurrection of the dead, the power of healing the lame, the blind, the deaf, and the dumb, of every disease and of every suffering—in a word, whosoever shall achieve this mystery, if he ask any of the things which I have just said unto you, they shall at once be granted unto him."

Hereupon the disciples cried out together in transport: "O Saviour, thou excitest us with very great frenzy because of the transcendent height which thou hast revealed unto us; and thou exaltest our souls, and they have become paths on which we travel to come unto thee, for they came forth from thee. Now, therefore, because of the transcendent heights which thou hast revealed unto us, our souls have come frenzied, and they travail mightily, yearning to go forth from us into the height to the region of thy kingdom."

The master continues his teaching, saying that the rest of the mysteries which have been committed unto them they may give to others, but not the mystery of the resurrection of the dead and the healing of disease, "for that mystery pertaineth to the rulers, it and all its namings." This they are to retain as the sign of their mission, so that when they do such wonder-deeds, "they will believe on you, that ye preach the God of perfection, and will have faith in all your words."

The next point of instruction taken up is the question: "Who constraineth a man to sin?" This opens up the whole subject of the constitution of man, and gives rise to a very interesting exposition of Gnostic psychology.

When the child is first born, the "light-power," "soul," "counterfeit spirit," and "body," are all very feeble in it. "None of them hath sense enough as yet for any work, whether good or evil, because of the exceeding great weight of oblivion."

The babe eateth of the delights of the world of the rulers; the power absorbeth from the portion of the power which is in the delights, the soul from the portion of the soul in the delights, the counterfeit spirit from the portion of evil in the delights, and the body from the unperceptive matter in the delights.

There is also another factor called the "destiny," which remains as it came into the world and takes nothing from the delights.

So, little by little, all these constituent elements in man develop, each sensing according to its nature. "The power senseth after the light of the height; the soul senseth after the region of mixed righteousness, which is the region of the mixture (of light and matter); and the counterfeit spirit seeketh after all vices, and desires, and sins; but the body hath no power of sensing unless it be an impulse to gain strength from matter."

The power is evidently the higher mind, the soul of the lower mind, and the counterfeit spirit the animal nature.

"The power within impelleth the soul to seek after the region of light and the whole godhead; whereas the counterfeit spirit draggeth down the soul, and persistently constraineth it to commit every kind of iniquity and mischief and sin, and persisteth as something foreign to the soul, and is its enemy, and maketh it commit all these sins and evils"—bringing them into operation against the soul because of what it has done in the past; moreover, for the future, "it spurreth on the workmen of wrath to bear witness to all the sin which it will constrain the soul to commit. And even when the man sleepeth by night or by day, it plagueth him in dreams with the desires of the world, and causeth him to long after all the things of this world. In a word, it bindeth the soul to all the actions which the rulers have decreed for it, and is the enemy of the soul, causing it to do what it would not." This it is which constraineth a man to sin.

The "destiny" is that which leadeth the man to his death. Then come the receivers of wrath to lead that soul out of the body.

"And for three days the receivers of wrath travel round with that soul through all the regions, taking it through all the aeons of the world; and the counterfeit spirit and destiny accompany that soul, but the power withdraws itself unto the virgin of light."

The soul is then brought down into chaos, and the counterfeit spirit becometh the receiver of that soul, and haunteth it, rebuking it in every punishment because of the sins which it hath caused it to commit; it is in exceeding great enmity to the soul.

The soul then rises higher, still always haunted by the counterfeit spirit, until it comes to the ruler of the way of the midst between the lower firmament and the earth-surface. Here it is still subjected to the punishments of its counterfeit spirit, according to its "destiny."

It is then brought by the counterfeit spirit to the "light of the sun"—the way of the midst being apparently the sublunary regions—and taken to the judge, the virgin of light, according to the commandment of Ieou, the first man; and "the virgin of light sealeth that soul and handeth it over to one of her receivers, and will have it carried into a body, which is the record of the sins which it hath committed."

"Amen, I say unto you she will not suffer that soul to escape from transmigrations into bodies, until it hath given signs of being in its last cycle according to its record of demerit."

In the case of a righteous soul, however, and one that hath received the higher mysteries of light, "when the time of that soul is come for its passing from the body, then the counterfeit spirit followeth after that soul; and also the destiny. They follow after it in the way whereby it shall pass into the height.

"And before it goeth far into the height, it uttereth the mystery of the breaking of the seals and all the bonds of the counterfeit spirit, whereby the rulers bind it to the soul"; and so they cease to impede the soul, and the destiny departeth to its own region, to the rulers of the way of the midst, and the counterfeit of the spirit to the rulers of the fate-sphere. And so it becometh a glorious light-stream and passeth up to its inheritance, for "the receivers of that soul, who pertain to the light, become wings of light for that soul," and will be a vesture of light for it. Such a soul requires no seals or apologies. . . .

Mary next enquires as to the nature of the mysteries of the baptisms which remit sins, and the Master replies:

"The counterfeit spirit beareth witness to every sin which the soul hath committed; not only doth it bear witness concerning the sins of the souls, but it sealeth every sin that it may be stamped on the soul, so that all the rulers of the punishments of sinners may know that it is the soul of a sinner, and may be informed of the number of sins which it hath committed, by the number of the seals which the counterfeit spirit hath stamped upon it, so that they may chastise it according to the number of sins which it hath committed. This is the fashion in which they treat the soul of the sinner.

"Now, therefore, when a man receiveth the mysteries of the baptisms, those mysteries become a mighty fire, exceedingly fierce, wise, which burneth up sins; they enter into the soul secretly and devour all the sins which the counterfeit spirit hath implanted in it.

"And when the fire hath purified all the sins which the counterfeit spirit hath implanted in the soul, the mysteries enter into the body occultly, that the fire may secretly pursue after the pursuers and cut them off with the body. They chase after the counterfeit spirit and the destiny, to separate them from the power and the soul, and place them with the body, so that the counterfeit spirit, the destiny, and the body may be separated into one group, and the soul and power into another. And the mystery of baptism remaineth between the two, and separateth the one from the other, in order that it may cleanse them and make them pure, that the soul and power may not be fouled in matter."

It is then further explained that all the twelve and other mysteries of the first mystery and of the ineffable are still higher than the mysteries of the baptisms; but all of this will be explained in a further teaching.

Mary gives interpretations of passages of scripture by the light of the new teaching, the opportunity being offered by a recapitulation of some of the points by the master, with enquiry as to whether they have well understood. Especially is the unending compassion of the highest mysteries insisted upon.

"If even a king of to-day, a man of the world, granteth boons unto them who are like unto him, if he moreover granteth pardon unto murderers, and them that are guilty of intercourse with males, and other horrible and capital crimes; if, I say, it is in the power even of one who is a man of the world to act thus, much more then have that ineffable and that first mystery, who are lords of the whole pleroma, power over everything to do as they will, and grant remission of sin unto every one who shall have received the mystery.

"Again, if even a king of to-day investeth a soldier with a royal mantle, and sendeth him to foreign regions, and the soldier there committeth murders and other grave offences worthy of death, and yet they are not brought home to him, because he weareth the royal mantle, how much more, then, [is it the case with] them who are mantled in the mysteries of the vestures of that ineffable, and those of the first mystery who are lords over all them of the height and all them of the depth!"

Thereupon the master makes trial of Peter, to see whether he is compassionate, in the case of a woman who had fallen away after receiving the mystery of baptism, and Peter comes out of the trial successfully.

It is then explained that the lot of a man who has received

the mysteries and fallen away and not repented, is far worse than that of the impious man who has never known them. As to those who are indifferent, thinking they have many births before them and need not hasten, the master bids the disciples:

"Preach ye unto the whole world, saying unto men: 'Strive together that ye may receive the mysteries of light in this time of stress, and enter into the kingdom of light. Put not off from day to day, and from cycle to cycle, in the belief that ye will succeed in obtaining the mysteries when ye return to the world in another cycle.'

"Such men know not when the number of perfect souls [shall be filled up]; for when the number of perfect souls shall be completed, I will then shut the gates of the light, and from that time none will be able to come in thereby, nor will any go forth thereafter, for the number of perfect souls shall be [completed], and the mystery of the First Mystery be perfected—[the mystery] whereby all hath come into existence, and I am that mystery.*

"From that hour no one shall any more enter into the light, and none shall come forth, in that the time of the number of perfect souls shall be fulfilled, before I set fire to the world, that it may purify the aeons, and veils, the firmaments and the whole world, and also all the matters that are still in it, the race of human kind being still upon it.

"At that time, then, the faith shall show itself forth more and more, and also the mysteries in those days. And many souls shall pass through the cycles of transmigrations of body and come back into the world in those days; and among them shall be some who are now alive and hear me teach concerning the consummation of the number of perfect souls, [and in those days] they shall find the mysteries of light, and shall receive them. They shall mount up to the gates of light, and shall find that the number of perfect souls is complete, which is the

* The doctrine of the contemporary sect which calls itself Jehovah's Witnesses, which proclaims the coming of the millennium when the number of perfect souls (who will constitute "the Bride of Christ") is made up, is reminiscent of this doctrine. —Ed.

consummation of the first mystery and the Gnosis of the pleroma; they will find that I have shut the gates of light, and that from that hour no one can come in or go forth thereby.

"Those souls then will cry within through the gates of light, saying: 'Master, open unto us.' And I will answer unto them, saying 'I know not whence ye are.' And they will say unto me, 'We have received the mysteries, and we have fulfilled all thy doctrine; thou didst teach us on the high ways.' And I will answer unto them, saying, 'I know not who ye are, ye who have practised iniquity and evil even unto this day. Wherefore go [hence] into the outer darkness.' Forthwith they will depart to the outer darkness, where there is weeping and gnashing of teeth."* . . .

The treatise ends with the following paragraphs:

"Mary answered and said: 'Blessed are we before all men because of these great [truths] which thou hast revealed unto us.'

"The Saviour answered and said unto Mary and all his disciples: 'I will also reveal unto you all the grandeurs of the height, from the interior of the interiors to the exterior of the exteriors, that ye may be perfect in every Gnosis, and in every pleroma, and in every height of the heights, and every deep of the depths.'

"And Mary answered and said to the Saviour: 'Now we know, O master, freely, surely, plainly, that thou hast brought the keys of the mysteries of the kingdom of light, which remit the sins of souls, that they may be cleansed, and be transformed into pure light, and be brought into the Light.'"[1]

SUMMARY OF THE EXTRACTS FROM THE BOOKS OF THE SAVIOR

One of the most highly prized manuscripts of Gnosticism is the Askew Codex, bought by the British Museum in the last quarter of the eighteenth century from the heirs of one Dr. Askew. It was written on vellum in Greek in the upper Egyptian dialect and consists of 346 quarto book pages. It contains

* Compare Matthew 8:12. —Ed.

*the strange document known as "Extracts from the Books of the
Savior," a condensed version of which follows. It would be a
hopeless task for this editor to try to interpret the meaning of
the work. Every reader, if he cares to try, must do this for
himself. Whatever the outcome he will do little, if any, worse
than the scholars, whose attempts have been futile. The many
brackets in the text indicate missing words in the ancient manuscript for which probable words or phrases have been inserted.*

"And they that are worthy of the mysteries which lie in
the ineffable, that is to say, those that have not emanated—
they are prior to the first mystery. To use a similitude and
correspondence of speech that ye may understand, they are
the limbs of the ineffable. And each is according to the dignity
of its glory, the head according to the dignity of the head, the
eye according to the dignity of the eye, the ear according
to the dignity of the ear, and the rest of the limbs (or members)
[in like fashion]; so that it is manifest that 'there are many
members, but only one body.' Of this I speak to you in a
paradigm, a correspondence, and a similitude, but not in the
reality of its configuration; I have not revealed the [whole]
word in truth.

"But the mystery of the ineffable and every limb which is in
it—that is to say, they that dwell in the mystery of the ineffable
and they that dwell in [that ineffable]—and also the three
spaces which follow after them, according to the mysteries, in
truth and verity, all that [is myself]. I am the treasure
of all of them, apart from which there is no treasure, apart from
which there is no individuality in the world; but there are other
words, other mysteries, and other regions.

"Now, therefore, blessed is he [among men] who hath found
the mysteries of the space towards the exterior. He is a god, who
hath found the words of the mysteries of the second space in the
midst. He is a saviour and free of every space who hath found
the words of the mysteries, the words of the third space
towards the interior. He is the very Pleroma itself (or more

excellent than the universe)—the object of desire of all who are in that third space—who hath found the mystery in which they [all] are, and in which they are [all] set. Wherefore is he equal to [all of them]. For he hath found also the words of the mysteries, which I have set down for you in a similitude, namely, the limbs of the ineffable. Amen, I say unto you, he who hath found the words of these mysteries in the truth of God that man is chief in the truth, he is its peer, because of these words and mysteries. The universe verily oweth its being to these words and mysteries. For which cause he who hath found the words of these mysteries, is equal to the chief [of all]. It is the gnosis of the Gnosis of the ineffable concerning which I speak unto you this day."

It came to pass, therefore, after they had crucified Jesus, our master, that he rose from the dead on the third day. And the disciples came together unto him and besought him, saying: "Master, have mercy upon us, for we have left father and mother, and the whole world, and have followed thee."

We are at once introduced to an atmosphere of ceremonies and invocations. Jesus stands by the Sea of the Ocean, surrounded by his disciples, male and female, and makes invocation with solemn prayer, saying: "Hear me, O Father, Father of all fatherhood, boundless light!" The prayer consists of the mystic vowels and formulae interspersed with "authentic" names.

The disciples are grouped round him, the women disciples stand behind, all clad in white linen robes; Jesus stands at an altar and with his disciples turns to the four quarters, invoking three times the name IAO. The interpretation of which is: "I, The pleroma hath gone forth; A, They shall return within; O, There shall be an end of ends."

This is followed by a mystic formula, which is interpreted as: "O Father of every fatherhood of the boundless [light-spaces], hear me because of my disciples, whom I have brought into thy presence, that they may believe in all the words of thy truth;

grant unto them all things for which I have cried unto thee, for I know the Name of the father of the treasure of light."

Then Jesus, whose mystery-name is Aberamentho, invokes the name of the Father of the Treasure, saying: "Let all the mysteries of the rulers, authorities, archangels, and all the powers and all the works of the invisible gods [their three mystery-names being given] withdraw themselves and roll themselves onto the right."

Thereupon all the lower regions speed to the west, to the left of the disk of the sun and of the moon.

The disk of the sun is symbolically described as a vast dragon with its tail in its mouth, mounted on seven powers, and drawn by four others figured as horses. The car of the moon is figured as a ship, its helms, or steering oars, being two dragons, male and female; it is drawn by two oxen, and steered by a babe on the poop, and at the prow is the face of a cat.

And Jesus and his disciples soar aloft into the aerial regions, the Way of the Midst, and come to the first order of the Way of the Midst.

Here the disciples are instructed on the nature of this space and its rulers. They are told that above them there are twelve aeons, six being ruled by Adamas and six by Iabraoth. The six under Iabraoth have repented and practised the mysteries of light, and have therefore been carried by Ieou, "the father of my father," to a pure atmosphere near the light of the sun. The six under Adamas have refused the mysteries of light, and persisted in the mystery of intercourse, or sexual union, and procreated rulers and archangels, and angels, workmen, and decans. They have accordingly been bound by Ieou in the fate-sphere. There are now three hundered and sixty of this brood, and again eighteen hundred ($1800=360\times5$) in each aeon. Over them Ieou has set five other great rulers, called in the world of human kind by these names: Kronos, Ares, Hermes, Aphrodite, and Zeus. Their incorruptible mystery-names and their genesis is also given.

Zeus is the head of the four, for Ieou reflected "that they had need of a helm to steer the world and the aeons of the spheres." Zeus is good, and passes three months in the revolutions of the remaining four ruling powers, "so that every ruler in which he cometh is freed from his iniquity." The peculiarity of Zeus is that he has two aeons for his habitation. . . .

[*There follows here a long, especially incomprehensible, discussion by Jesus of "the mystery of the twelve aeons of the rulers, their seals, their numbers, and the manner of invocation to enter into their regions," etc., which has been omitted.—Ed.*]

And when the disciples had heard this, they bowed down and adored him, saying: "Save us, O Master, have mercy upon us, that we may be preserved from these malignant torments which are prepared for sinners. Woe unto them! woe unto the children of men! for they are like the blind feeling in the darkness, and seeing not. Have mercy upon us, O master, in the great blindness in which we are, and have mercy upon the whole race of human kind; for they lie in wait for their souls, as lions for their prey, to tear them in pieces and make food for their torments, because of the forgetfulness and ignorance in which they are. Have mercy, therefore, upon us, O master, our Saviour, have mercy upon us, preserve us from this great stupor!"

Jesus said unto his disciples: "Have courage, fear not, for ye are blessed: nay, I will make you lords over all these, and place them in subjection under your feet. Ye remember that I have already said unto you before my crucifixion: 'I will give unto you the keys of the kingdom of the heavens.' [Matthew 16:19.] Now again I say unto you, I will give them unto you."

When Jesus had thus spoken, he chanted an invocation in the great name, and the regions of the ways of the midst were hidden from view and Jesus and his disciples remained in an atmosphere of exceeding great light.

Jesus said unto his disciples: "Come unto me." And they came unto him. He turned towards the four angles of the world; he uttered the great name over their heads, and blessed them and breathed on their eyes. Jesus said unto them: "Look up, and mark what ye see!"

They said: "We see fire and water, and wine and blood."

Jesus, that is to say Aberamentho, said unto his disciples: "Amen, I say unto you, I have brought nothing into the world when I came, save this fire and water, this wine and blood. I brought down the water and fire from the region of the light of light, from the treasure of light; I brought down the wine and the blood from the region of Barbelo. And shortly after my father sent unto me the holy spirit in the form of a dove.

"The fire, the water, and the wine are for cleansing all the sins of the world: the blood I had as a sign of the body of human kind, and I received it in the region of Barbelo, the great power of the Divine Invisible; while the spirit draweth all souls and bringeth them into the region of light."

This is the "fire" he came to "cast on the earth" according to a former saying; this the "living water" the Samaritan woman should have asked for; this the "cup of wine" in the eucharist; this the "water" that came from his side.

"These are the mysteries of the light which remit sins"—that is to say, their names merely.

After this Jesus again gives the command that the powers of the left return to their own region, and the disciples find themselves once more on the Mount of Galilee.

Hereupon Jesus celebrates the mystic eucharist and the first baptism of water, with ceremonies and invocations almost identical to those in the Codex Brucianus. The disciples enquire further as to the nature of the baptism of incense, the baptism of the Holy Spirit, and the spiritual chrism, and ask that the "mystery of the light of thy father" be revealed to them.

Jesus said unto them: "As to these mysteries which ye seek after, there is no mystery which is higher than them. They will bring your souls into the light of lights, into the regions of truth and righteousness, into the region of the holy of all holies, into the region where there is neither female nor male, nor form in that region, but only light, unceasing, ineffable.

"No mystery is higher than the mysteries ye seek after, save only the mystery of the seven voices and their nine-and-forty powers and numbers; and the name which is higher than them all, the name which sums up all their names, all their lights, and all their powers."[2]

THE GOSPEL OF TRUTH

Until about 1945 this apocryphal book was known only through comments concerning it by Irenaeus and Tertullian. However, what appears to be a complete copy of it, translated from Greek into Coptic—apparently about the middle of the fourth century A.D. was discovered near Nag Hammadi. It is now in the possession of the Jung Institute in Zurich. Its apparent purpose is to say that the entire message of Jesus is summed up in the "Gnosis"—the secret knowledge contained in the Gnostic mysteries, and that one who has mastered this "Gnosis" will be freed from his earth-born shackles and ascend to the fullness of being. Make what you can of it. As in the "Extracts from the Books of the Savior," the material in brackets probably consists of additions in places where the manuscript was damaged, or the translation uncertain.

The Gospel of Truth is joy for those who have received from the Father of truth the grace of knowing him through the power of the Word, which has come forth from the Pleroma,* which is in the thought and mind of the Father [and] which is he whom they call "the Saviour," for that is the name of the work which he is to accomplish for the salvation of those who were ignorant of the Father; and this name "the Gospel" is the revelation of hope, since it is a discovery for those who seek him. . . .

Ignorance concerning the Father produced anguish and terror.

---

* Here the word "Pleroma," which in other texts has been translated as "the fullness," is translated as "the Word"—apparently the meaning of the Greek *Logos*, translated "the Word" in the Gospel according to John. —Ed.

And the anguish became dense like a mist, so that no one could see. For this reason Error waxed strong. . . .

[The works of Error, designed to "lead astray those of the Midst and take them captive," involve no humiliation for the Father, nor do they come from him. They are as nothing, whereas the truth is "unalterable, unshakable, and of a beauty which cannot be improved upon." What did come from the Father was knowledge, "which was manifested in order that oblivion might be done away and that (men) might know the Father." As soon as men come to this knowledge, "oblivion" (which is ignorance of God) will no longer exist, and this is the Gospel revealed to the perfect. Here the author refers to the ministry of Jesus, who] enlightened those who were in darkness by reason of oblivion. He enlightened them. He gave them a way. And the way is the truth which he taught them. Because of this Error was wroth with him, persecuted him, oppressed him, brought him to naught. He was nailed to a tree, and became a fruit of the knowledge of the Father. . . .

In the place of instruction he came in the midst, he spake the word as a master. There came to him those who were wise in their own estimation, putting him to the proof; but he confounded them, for they were foolish. They hated him, for they were not truly wise men. After all these there came to him the little children, those to whom belongs the knowledge of the Father. . . .

There was manifested in their heart the living book of the living, which is written in the thought and [in] the mind of the Father and which from before the foundation of the All was in that part of him which is incomprehensible, this [book] . . . none has power to take, since that is reserved for him who shall take it and shall be slain. No one could become manifest of those who believed in the salvation, so long as that book had not made its appearance. For this reason the merciful and faithful Jesus was compassionate, he accepted the sufferings until he took that book, since he knew that his death is life for many. . . .

He was nailed to a tree [and] he affixed the ordinance of the Father to the cross. O, what a great teaching! He humbles himself even unto death though clothed with immortal life. Having divested himself of these perishable rags, he clothed himself with incorruptibility, which it is impossible for anyone to take away from him. . . .

Therefore if anyone possesses knowledge, he receives that which is his own and draws it back to himself. For he who is ignorant is deficient, and it is a great thing which he lacks, since he lacks what will make him perfect. Since the perfection of the All is in the Father, it is necessary that the All ascend to him, and that each one receive that which is his own, [the things] which he has written down beforehand, having prepared them to be given to those who came forth from him. Those whose names he knew beforehand are called at the end, so that he who knows is he whose name the Father has pronounced. For he whose name has not been pronounced is ignorant. Indeed, how should anyone hear, if his name has not been called? For he who remains ignorant to the end is a creature of oblivion, and will be destroyed with it. . . .

If anyone possesses knowledge, he is a being from on high. If he is called, he hears, replies, and turns towards him who calls him in order to ascend to him, and he knows in what way he is called. Since he knows, he performs the will of him who called him. He desires to please him [and] receives rest. . . .

He who thus possesses knowledge knows whence he is come and whither he is going. He knows even as a person who, having been intoxicated, has recovered from his intoxication, and having come to himself sets in order the things that belong to him. . . .

Thus the word of the Father proceeds forth into the All, being the fruit of his heart and a form of his will. It upholds the All, it chooses it, and also takes [upon itself] the form of the All, purifying it and causing it to return to the Father and to the Mother, Jesus of the infinite gentleness. The Father reveals his breast; but his breast is the Holy Spirit. He reveals that of Himself which was hidden [that of himself which was hidden was his Son] in order that through the compassion of the Father the aeons might know him, and cease to torment themselves in search of the Father, resting in him since they know that this is rest. When he had filled up the deficiency he abolished the form. His form is the world, that wherein he served. For where there is envy and dissension, there is deficiency; but where there is unity, there is perfection. Since deficiency came into existence because they did not know the Father, so when they know the Father deficiency from that moment will no longer exist. Just as in the case of anyone's ignorance, at the moment when he comes to know his ignorance disappears of its own accord; just as the darkness dissolves when the light appears, so also the deficiency is dissolved by the perfection. . . .

[By means of knowledge each] will purify himself from diversity into unity, devouring the matter within him like a fire, darkness by light, death by life. If then these things have happened to each one of us, it is fitting for us to take thought above all that the house may be holy and silent for the Unity. . . .

[Here the author introduces an analogy of unsound vessels which are smashed by their owners and replaced by sound ones. This, he says,] is the judgment come from above, which has judged every man, a drawn sword with double edge which cuts on one side and on the other. When the Word appeared . . . a great confusion arose among the vessels, for some had been emptied, others filled; for lo, some were provided for, others were overturned; some were purified, others were broken to pieces. . . .

What then is that which he desires that [man] should think? This: "I am become like the shadows and the phantoms of the night." When the light dawns upon the terror which had laid hold of him, that man knows that it is nothing. . . .

[The state of the "ignorant" is vividly portrayed, "as if they were sunk in sleep and found themselves a prey to troubled dreams."] Either it is a place to which they are fleeing, or they are powerless when they have been in pursuit of someone; or they are involved in brawls, or they are themselves receiving blows; or they are falling from great heights, or they fly off into the air, even though they have no wings. At other times again it is as if someone were trying to kill them, although there is no one pursuing them, or they themselves were killing those near to them, for they are defiled with their blood. Up to the time when those who pass through all these things wake up, they see nothing, those who were in all these confusions, for they were nothing. So it is with those who have cast ignorance away from them, like sleep, because they reckon (it) as nothing. . . .

[The works of ignorance are abandoned "like a dream in the night." The knowledge of the Father, on the other hand, "they esteem as the light." To receive *gnosis* is like awaking from sleep. The Spirit gives to men the possibility of knowing "the knowledge of the Father and the revelation of his Son."]

For when they had seen and heard him, he allowed them to taste him and to smell him, and to lay hold of the beloved Son. He appeared, instructing them about the Father, the incomprehensible. He breathed into them that which is in the thought, accomplishing his will. Many received the light and turned to him. . . .

The Light spoke through his mouth, and his voice engendered life. He gave them thought and understanding, compassion and deliverance and the Spirit of power from the boundlessness and sweetness of the Father. He caused the punishments and torments to cease, for it was they which caused many in need of mercy to wander from him in error and in chains; and with power he destroyed them, and he put them to shame through knowledge. He became a way for those who erred, and knowledge for those who were ignorant; a discovery for those who sought, and strength for those who wavered; spotlessness for those who were defiled. He is the shepherd who abandoned the ninety-nine sheep which had not gone astray. He went in search of that one which had strayed. He rejoiced when he found it. For ninety-nine is a number which is in the left hand, which encompasses it. But as soon as the one is found the whole number passes over to the right [hand]. Thus it is with him who lacks the one, that is to say, the entire right hand, which attracts that which is lacking and takes it away from the left side, and passes over to the right; and in this way the number becomes a hundred. . . . Even on the Sabbath he laboured for the sheep, which he found fallen into a pit. He preserved the sheep alive by bringing it out of the pit, that you may understand—you, the children of understanding—what is that Sabbath on which it is not fitting that redemption remain inactive; that you may speak of that day which is above, wherein there is no night; and of the light which does not pass away, because it is perfect. Speak, then, from your hearts, for you are this perfect day, and in you dwells the light which has no end. . . .

For the children of the Father, they are his fragrance, since they are from the grace of his countenance. Because of this the Father loves his fragrance, and makes it manifest in every place; and if it be mixed with matter, he gives his fragrance to the light and in his silence he causes it to rise above every form and every sound. For it is not the ears which smell the fragrance, but it is the spirit which has the [faculty of] smelling, and it draws it itself, and plunges down into the fragrance of the Father. . . .

Because of this, faith came. It destroyed the separation and brought the warm fulness of love; in order that the cold might not come again into existence, but the unity of the perfect thought. This is the word of the glad tidings of the coming of the fulness for those who are awaiting the salvation that comes from above. . . .

For this reason Imperishability breathed forth. It followed after him who had sinned, that he might find rest. . . . For the physician hastens to the place where there is a sick [man], for that is the desire that is in him. He then who suffers lack hides it not, for he [the physician] has what he [the sick man] needs. Thus the pleroma, which does not lack, fills up the deficiency, [the pleroma] which he [the Father] gave of himself to fill up what he needs, in order that he might receive grace; for at the time when he was deficient he did not possess grace. . . .

But the will is that in which the Father rests and which pleases him. Nothing comes to pass without him, nor does anything occur without the will of the Father. But incomprehensible is his will. . . .

[It is the Father] from whom the beginning came forth and to whom shall return all those who came forth from him. But they were manifested for the glory and the joy of his name. But the name of the Father is the Son. He it is who in the beginning gave a name to him who came forth from him, and who was himself, and whom he engendered as a Son. He gave him his name which belonged to him, since he it is, even the Father, to whom belong all things which are with him. He has the name, he has the Son. It is possible for them to see him. But the name, on the contrary, is invisible, since it alone is the mystery of the Invisible, which comes to ears which are all filled with it. For indeed one does not pronounce the name of the Father, but he is revealed in a son. . . .

The first thing we must do, then, is to understand this point: "What is the Name?" For it is the true name. It is indeed the name which came from the Father, for it is he who is Lord of the name. Now he received the name not by way of loan, like others, according to the manner in which every one is equipped. But he is Lord of the name. There is no other to whom he has given it. But it is unnameable (and) ineffable until the moment when he alone who is perfect pronounced it; and he it is who has power to pronounce his name and to see it. . . .

He will speak about the place from which each one has come, and [each] will hasten to return once more to the region from which he derived his true condition, and to be delivered from that place, the place wherein he has been, since he tastes of that place and receives nourishment and growth [therein]. And his own place of rest is his pleroma. All the emanations of the Father, then, are pleromas, and all his emanations have their root in him who caused them all to grow from himself and gave to them their destiny.

The place to which they direct their thoughts, that place is their root, which lifts them up through all the heights to the Father. . . .

Neither did they disparage the glory of the Father, nor did they think of him as small; nor that he is harsh, nor that he is wrathful; but he is absolutely good, unshakable, mild, knowing all the spaces even before they have come into existence, and having no need of instruction. This is the manner of those who have something from on high, through this immeasurable greatness, in that they strain towards that unique one who is perfect and who is there for their sakes. And they do not descend into Hades, nor have they any jealousy or sighing, nor is there any death among them, but they rest in him who rests. They labour not, neither are they entangled in the search for the truth, but they are themselves the truth. And the Father is in them, and they are in the Father, perfect and inseparable from that truly good [Being].

This is the place of the blessed; this is their place. As for the rest, let them consider in their places that it is not befitting for me, after I have been in the place of rest, to speak of anything else. But therein shall I be, and devote myself at all times to the Father of the All, and to the true brethren, upon whom the love of the Father is poured out, and in whose midst nothing of him is lacking. These are they who are manifest in truth, since they are in that true and eternal life, and speak of the light that is perfect and filled with the seed of the Father, and which is in his heart and in the pleroma, while his Spirit re-joices in him and glorifies him in whom it was, for he is good. And his children are perfect, and worthy of his name, for it is children of this kind that he, the Father, loves.[3]

9

THE FATE OF PONTIUS PILATE

For obvious reasons, the fate of Pontius Pilate, the Roman governor who condemned Jesus to the cross, was of great interest to the early Christians. The first of the apocryphal stories we shall quote in this chapter is from The Acts of Pilate, which, as previously noted, is probably a fourth-century document.

THE REGRET OF PILATE

After these things [that is, the crucifixion and reports of the resurrection] Pilate entered into the temple of the Jews and gathered together all the chief of the priests, and the teachers and scribes and doctors of the law, and went in with them into the holy place of the temple and commanded all the doors to be shut, and said unto them: "We have heard that ye have in this temple a certain great Bible; wherefore I ask you that it be presented before us."

And when that great Bible adorned with gold and precious jewels was brought by four ministers, Pilate said to them all: "I adjure you by the God of your fathers which commanded you to build this temple in the place of his sanctuary, that ye hide not the truth from me. Ye know all the things that are written in this Bible; but tell me now if ye have found in the scriptures that this Jesus whom ye have crucified is the Son of God which should come for the salvation of mankind, and in what year of the times he must come. Declare unto me whether ye crucified him in ignorance or knowingly."

And Annas and Caiaphas when they were thus adjured commanded all the rest that were with them to go out of the temple; and they themselves shut all the doors of the temple and of the sanctuary, and said unto Pilate: "Thou hast adjured us, O excellent judge, by the building of this temple to make manifest unto thee the truth and reason. After that we had crucified Jesus, knowing not that he was the Son of God, but supposing that by some chance he did his wondrous works, we made a great assembly in this temple; and as we conferred one with another concerning the signs of the mighty works which Jesus had done, we found many witnesses of our own nation who said that they had seen Jesus alive after his passion, and that he was passed into the height of the heaven.

"Moreover, we saw two witnesses whom Jesus raised from the dead, who declared unto us many marvellous things which Jesus did among the dead, which things we have in writing in our hands. Now our custom is that every year before our assembly we open this holy Bible and inquire the testimony of God. And we have found in the first book of the Seventy how that Michael the angel spake unto the third son of Adam the first man concerning the five thousand and five hundred years, wherein should come the most beloved Son of God, even Christ: and furthermore we have thought that peradventure this same was the God of Israel which said unto Moses: Make thee an ark of the covenant in length two cubits and a half, and in breadth one cubit and a half, and in height one cubit and a half. For by those five cubits and a half we have understood and known the fashion of the ark of the old covenant, for that in five thousand and a half thousand years Jesus Christ should come in the ark of his body; and we have found that he is the God of Israel, even the Son of God.

"For after his passion, we the chief of the priests, because we marvelled at the signs which came to pass on his account, did open the Bible, and searched out all the generations unto the generation of Joseph, and Mary the mother of Christ, taking her to be the seed of David: and we found that from the day when

God made the heaven and the earth and the first man, from that time unto the Flood are 2,212 years: and from the Flood unto the building of the tower 531 years: and from the building of the tower unto Abraham 606 years: and from Abraham unto the coming of the children of Israel out of Egypt 470 years: and from the going of the children of Israel out of Egypt unto the building of the temple 511 years: and from the building of the temple unto the destruction of the same temple 464 years: so far found we in the Bible of Esdras: and inquiring from the burning of the temple unto the coming of Christ and his birth we found it to be 636 years, which together were five thousand and five hundred years, like as we found it written in the Bible that Michael the archangel declared before unto Seth the third son of Adam, that after five thousand and a half thousand years Christ the Son of God should come.

"Hitherto have we told no man, lest there should be a schism in our synagogues; and now, O excellent judge, thou hast adjured us by this holy Bible of the testimonies of God, and we do declare it unto thee: and we also have adjured thee by thy life and health that thou declare not these words unto any man in Jerusalem."

And Pilate, when he heard these words of Annas and Caiaphas, laid them all up amongst the acts of the Lord and Saviour in the public books of his judgement hall, and wrote a letter unto Claudius the king of the city of Rome, saying:

Pontius Pilate unto Claudius, greeting:

There befell of late a matter which I myself brought to light: for the Jews through envy have punished themselves and their posterity with fearful judgements of their own fault; for whereas their fathers had promises that their God would send them out of heaven his holy one who should of right be called their king, and did promise that he would send him upon earth by a virgin; he, then, came when I was governor of Judaea, and they beheld him enlightening the blind, cleansing lepers, healing the palsied, driving devils out of men, raising the dead, rebuking the winds, walking upon the waves of the sea dry-shod, and doing many

other wonders, and all the people of the Jews calling him the
Son of God: the chief priests therefore, moved with envy
against him, took him and delivered him unto me and brought
against him one false accusation after another, saying that he
was a sorcerer and did things contrary to their law.

But I, believing that these things were so, having scourged
him, delivered him unto their will: and they crucified him, and
when he was buried they set guards upon him. But while my
soldiers watched him he rose again on the third day: yet so
much was the malice of the Jews kindled that they gave money
to the soldiers, saying: "Say ye that his disciples stole away his
body."

But they, though they took the money, were not able to keep
silence concerning that which had come to pass, for they also
have testified that they saw him arisen and that they received
money from the Jews. And these things have I reported (unto
thy mightiness) for this cause, lest some other should lie *unto
thee* [Lat., lest any lie otherwise] and thou shouldest deem
right to believe the false tales of the Jews.[1]

CORRESPONDENCE OF PILATE WITH OTHERS

*"Appendixes to The Acts of Pilate" seems to be an arbitrary
title that has been used to refer to various forms of reports
attributed to Pilate, and letters—whether any of them are gen-
uine or not is unknown. It is probable that they were written by
others, though Tertullian, a father of the African church of the
second and third centuries, stated as a fact that Pilate had
made a report to Tiberius, and that the latter tried, without
success, to induce the Roman Senate to declare Jesus a god.
The texts from which selections have been taken are late, and,
of course, untrustworthy as history. Yet they seem worth per-
petuating if only as evidence of a desire in some sections of
early Christianity to emphasize the hesitation shown by Pilate
to have Jesus crucified, that is evident in the canonical gospels,
and to add to the story an ending in which Pilate suffered*

what the Church felt was a just punishment for his part in the death of Jesus of Nazareth.

LETTER OF PILATE TO TIBERIUS

Jesus Christ of whom I recently wrote to you has been executed against my will. So pious and austere a man has never been seen, nor will be again. But there was a wonderful unanimity in the request of the Jews and their leader that he should be crucified, though their own prophets, and the Sibyls, testified against them, and signs appeared at his death which the philosophers said threatened the collapse of the whole world. His disciples who still live do not belie their master's teaching, but are active in good works. Had I not feared a general rising, the man might have been yet alive.

REPORT OF PILATE

Jesus was delivered to him by Herod, Archelaus, Philip, Annas, Caiaphas, and all the people.

At his crucifixion the sun was darkened; the stars appeared, and in all the world people lighted lamps from the sixth hour till evening; the moon appeared like blood, and the stars and Orion lamented at the sin of the Jews. [The other recension says that Abraham, Isaac, Jacob, the twelve patriarchs, and Moses and Job, who were seen by the Jews, and many others "whom I, too, saw," appeared in the body and thus lamented.]

On the first day of the week, at the third hour of night, there was a great light: the sun shone with unwonted brightness, men in shining garments appeared in the air and cried out to the souls in Hades to come up, and proclaimed the resurrection of Jesus.

The light continued all night. Many Jews disappeared in the chasms which the earthquake had caused: and all the synagogues except one fell down.

Under the stress of the consternation caused by all these
portents Pilate writes to Caesar.

To this is appended in one recension the "Delivering up,
Paradosis, of Pilate."

On receipt of the letter there was great astonishment at
Rome, and Caesar in wrath ordered Pilate to be brought to
him as a prisoner.

On hearing of his arrival Caesar took his seat "in the temple
of the gods before all the senate, and with all his army and all
the multitude of his power," and said to Pilate: How didst thou
dare, thou, most impious, to do such a thing, when thou hadst
seen such signs concerning that man? by thy wicked daring thou
hast destroyed the whole world.

Pilate threw the blame on the Jews, on Herod, Archelaus,
Philip, Annas, and Caiaphas. Caesar. Why didst thou yield to
them? Pilate. The nation is rebellious and disobedient. Caesar.
Thou oughtest to have kept him safe and sent him to me, and
not have yielded and crucified one who had done all those
mighty works of which thou spakest in thy report. It is plain
that he was the Christ, the king of the Jews.

When Caesar named Christ, all the images of the gods fell
down and became as dust. There was great consternation:
Caesar remanded Pilate to prison.

Next day he sat in the Capitol with all the senate, and a
dialogue similar to the last took place. After it Caesar wrote to
Licianus, the chief governor of the East, bidding him enslave all
the nation of the Jews, and make them few in number for their
wickedness. This Licianus did.

Caesar then commanded a ruler named Albius to behead
Pilate. He was led forth to death, and prayed: Number me not
among the wicked Hebrews. Remember not evil against me or
against thy servant Procla which standeth here, whom thou
didst make to prophesy that thou must be nailed to the cross.
But pardon us and number us among thy righteous ones.

LETTER OF PILATE TO HEROD

It was no good thing which I did at your persuasion when I crucified Jesus. I ascertained from the centurion and the soldiers that he rose again, and I sent to Galilee and learned that he was preaching there to above five hundred believers.

My wife Procla took Longinus, the believing centurion, and ten soldiers who had kept the sepulchre, and went forth and found him "sitting in a tilled field" teaching a multitude. He saw them, addressed them, and spoke of his victory over death and hell. Procla and the rest returned and told me. I was in great distress, and put on a mourning garment and went with her and fifty soldiers to Galilee. We found Jesus: and as we approached him there was a sound in heaven and thunder, and the earth trembled and gave forth a sweet odour. We fell on our faces and the Lord came and raised us up, and I saw on him the scars of the passion, and he laid his hands on my shoulders, saying: "All generations and families shall call thee blessed because in thy days the Son of Man died and rose again."

LETTER OF HEROD TO PILATE

It is in no small sorrow—according to the divine Scriptures—that I write to you.

My dear daughter Herodias was playing upon the water and fell in up to her neck. And her mother caught at her head to save her, and it was cut off, and the water swept her body away. My wife is sitting with the head on her knees, weeping, and all the house is full of sorrow.

I am in great distress of mind at the death of Jesus, and reflecting on my sins in killing John Baptist and massacring the Innocents. Since, then, you are able to see the man Jesus again, strive for me and intercede for me: for to you Gentiles the kingdom is given, according to the prophets and Christ.

Lesbonax my son is in the last stages of a decline. I am afflicted with dropsy, and worms are coming out of my mouth. My wife's left eye is blinded through weeping. Righteous are the judgements of God, because we mocked at the eye of the righteous. Vengeance will come on the Jews and the priests, and the Gentiles will inherit the kingdom, and the children of light be cast out.

And, Pilate, since we are of one age, bury my family honourably; it is better for us to be buried by you than by the priests, who are doomed to speedy destruction. Farewell. I have sent you my wife's earrings and my own signet ring. I am already beginning to receive judgement in this world, but I fear the judgement hereafter much more. This is temporary, that is everlasting.

LETTER OF TIBERIUS TO PILATE

This was delivered to Pilate by means of the messenger Raab, who was sent with 2,000 soldiers to bring him to Rome.

"Since you have given a violent and iniquitous sentence of death against Jesus of Nazareth, showing no pity, and having received gifts to condemn him, and with your tongue have expressed sympathy, but in your heart have delivered him up, you shall be brought home a prisoner to answer for yourself.

"I have been exceedingly distressed at the reports that have reached me: a woman, a disciple of Jesus, has been here, called Mary Magdalene, out of whom he is said to have cast seven devils, and has told of all his wonderful cures. How could you permit him to be crucified? If you did not receive him as a God, you might at least have honoured him as a physician. Your own deceitful writing to me has condemned you.

"As you unjustly sentenced him, I shall justly sentence you, and your accomplices as well."[2]

THE DEATH OF PILATE

Pilate, Archelaus, Philip, Annas, and Caiaphas were arrested. Rachaab and the soldiers slew all the Jewish males, defiled the women, and brought the leaders to Rome. On the way Caiaphas died in Crete: the earth would not receive his body, and he was covered with a cairn of stones.

It was the old law that if a condemned criminal saw the face of the emperor he was spared: so Tiberius would not see Pilate, but shut him up in a cave.

Annas was sewed into a fresh bull's-hide, which, contracting as it dried, squeezed him to death. The other chiefs of the Jews were beheaded: Archelaus and Philip were crucified.

One day the emperor went out to hunt, and chased a hind to the door of Pilate's prison. Pilate looked out, trying to see the emperor's face, but at that moment the emperor shot an arrow at the hind, which went in at the window and killed Pilate.[3]

There is another version of the story of the death of Pilate from the same source. It follows:

Pilate was arrested and brought before the emperor of Rome. Now he was wearing the seamless tunic of Jesus. When he came before the emperor, he, who had been raging against him before, became quite mild. He sent Pilate away and immediately his rage returned. This happened again. Then, either by divine inspiration or on the suggestion of some Christian, he had him stripped of the tunic, sent him back to prison, and shortly after sentenced him to die by the basest of deaths. On hearing this, Pilate killed himself with his own knife. Caesar had a millstone tied to his neck and threw him into the Tiber. The demons gathered in crowds, and storms disturbed the place so that all were in great fear. The corpse was taken out of the river and carried off to Vienne (via Gehennae) on the Rhone, with the same result. Thence it was taken to be buried in the territory of Lausanne; but disturbances continued there till the inhabitants dug it up and threw it into a well surrounded by mountains, where diabolical manifestations are still said to occur.[4]

10

——◆——

LAST WORDS

The Epistle of the Apostles, also known as the Testament of our Lord in Galilee, with which this book closes, is believed to be the work of an orthodox Catholic of Asia Minor of about A.D. 160, though very few traces of its use in churches have been discovered. It was apparently written as a refutation of Gnostic doctrine.

The book which Jesus Christ revealed unto his disciples: and how that Jesus Christ revealed the book for the apostles, the disciples of Jesus Christ, even the book which is for all men. Simon and Cerinthus, the false apostles, concerning whom it is written that no man shall cleave unto them, for there is in them deceit wherewith they bring men to destruction. The book hath been written that ye may be steadfast and not flinch nor be troubled, and depart not from the word of the Gospel which ye have heard. Like as we heard it, we keep it in remembrance and have written it for the whole world. We commend you our sons and our daughters in joy to the grace of God in the name of God the Father the Lord of the world, and of Jesus Christ. Let grace be multiplied upon you.

We, John, Thomas, Peter, Andrew, James, Philip, Bartholomew, Matthew, Nathanael, Judas Zelotes, and Cephas, write unto the churches of the east and the west, of the north and the south, declaring and imparting unto you that which concerneth our Lord Jesus Christ: we do write according as we have seen and heard and touched him, after that he was risen from the dead; and how that he revealed unto us things mighty and wonderful and true.

This know we: that our Lord and Redeemer Jesus Christ is God the Son of God, who was sent of God the Lord of the whole world, the maker and creator of it, who is named by all names, and high above all powers, Lord of lords, King of kings, Ruler of rulers, the heavenly one, that sitteth above the cherubim and seraphim at the right hand of the throne of the Father: who by his word made the heavens, and formed the earth and that which is in it, and set bounds to the sea that it should not pass: the deeps also and fountains, that they should spring forth and flow over the earth: the day and the night, the sun and the moon, did he establish, and the stars in the heaven: that did separate the light from the darkness: that called forth hell, and in the twinkling of an eye ordained the rain of the winter, the snow, the hail, and the ice, and the days in their several seasons: that maketh the earth to quake and again establisheth it: that created man in his own image, after his likeness, and by the fathers of old and the prophets is it declared, of whom the apostles preached, and whom the disciples did touch. In God, the Lord, the Son of God, do we believe, that he is the word become flesh: that of Mary the holy virgin he took a body, begotten of the Holy Ghost, not of the will of the flesh, but by the will of God: that he was wrapped in swaddling clothes in Bethlehem and made manifest, and grew up and came to ripe age, when also we beheld it. . . .

And thereafter when we had no bread, but only five loaves and two fishes, he commanded the people to sit them down, and the number of them was five thousand, besides children and women. We did set pieces of bread before them, and they ate and were filled, and there remained over, and we filled twelve baskets full of the fragments, asking one another and saying: "What mean these five loaves? They are the symbol of our faith in the Lord of the Christians, even in the Father, the Lord Almighty, and in Jesus Christ our redeemer, in the Holy

Ghost the comforter, in the holy church, and in the remission of sins."

These things did our Lord and Saviour reveal unto us and teach us. And we do even as he, that ye may become partakers in the grace of our Lord and in our ministry and our giving of thanks, and think upon life eternal. Be ye steadfast and waver not in the knowledge and confidence of our Lord Jesus Christ, and he will have mercy on you and save you everlastingly, world without end.

Cerinthus and Simon are come to go to and fro in the world, but they are enemies of our Lord Jesus Christ, for they do pervert the word and the true thing, even Jesus Christ. Keep yourselves therefore far from them, for death is in them, and great pollution and corruption, even in these on whom shall come judgement and the end and everlasting destruction.

Therefore have we not shrunk from writing unto you concerning the testimony of Christ our Saviour, of what he did, when we followed with him, how he enlightened our understanding. . . .

Concerning whom we testify that the Lord is he who was crucified by Pontius Pilate and Archelaus between the two thieves and with them he was taken down from the tree of the cross, and was buried in a place which is called the place of a skull. And thither went three women, Mary, she that was kin to Martha, and Mary Magdalene, and took ointments to pour upon the body, weeping and mourning over that which was come to pass. And when they drew near to the sepulchre, they looked in and found not the body.

And as they mourned and wept, the Lord showed himself unto them and said to them: "For whom weep ye? weep no more, I am he whom ye seek. But let one of you go to your brethren and say: 'Come ye, the Master is risen from the dead.'"

Martha came and told us. We said unto her: "What have we to do with thee, woman? He that is dead and buried, is it possible that he should live?" And we believed her not that the Saviour was risen from the dead.

Then she returned unto the Lord and said unto him: "None of them hath believed me, that thou livest."

He said: "Let another of you go unto them and tell them again." Mary came and told us again, and we believed her not; and she returned unto the Lord and she also told him.

Then said the Lord unto Mary and her sisters: "Let us go unto them."

And he came and found us within, and called us out; but we thought that it was a phantom and believed not that it was the Lord. Then said he unto us: "Come, fear ye not. I am your master, even he, O Peter, whom thou didst deny thrice; and dost thou now deny again?"

And we came unto him, doubting in our hearts whether it were he. Then said he unto us: "Wherefore doubt ye still, and are unbelieving? I am he that spake unto you of my flesh and my death and my resurrection. But that ye may know that I am he, do thou, Peter, put thy finger into the print of the nails in mine hands, and thou also, Thomas, put thy finger into the wound of the spear in my side; but thou, Andrew, look on my feet and see whether they press the earth; for it is written in the prophet: 'A phantom of a devil maketh no footprint on the earth.'"

And we touched him, that we might learn of a truth whether he were risen in the flesh; and we fell on our faces and worshipped him confessing our sin, that we had been unbelieving. Then said our Lord and Saviour unto us: "Rise up, and I will reveal unto you that which is above the heaven and in the heaven, and your rest which is in the kingdom of heaven. For my Father hath given me power to take you up thither, and them also that believe on me."

Now that which he revealed unto us is this, which he spake: "It came to pass when I was about to come hither from the Father of all things, and passed through the heavens, then did I put on the wisdom of the Father, and I put on the power of his might. I was in heaven, and I passed by the archangels and the angels in their likeness, like as if I were one of them, among the princedoms and powers. I passed through them because I possessed the wisdom of him that had sent me. . . . And so wrought I the likeness by my wisdom; for I became all things in all, that I might praise the dispensation of the Father and fulfil the glory of him that sent me and return unto him." . . .

And we answered: "Yea, Lord."

"But do ye commemorate my death. Now when the Passover cometh, one of you shall be cast into prison for my name's sake; and he will be in grief and sorrow, because ye keep the Easter while he is in prison and separated from you, for he will be sorrowful because he keepeth not Easter with you. And I will send my power in the form of mine angel Gabriel, and the doors of the prison shall open. And he shall come forth and come unto you and keep the night-watch with you until the cock crow. And when ye have accomplished the memorial which is made of me, and the Agape [love-feast], he shall again be cast into prison for a testimony, until he shall come out thence and preach that which I have delivered unto you."

And we said unto him: "Lord, is it then needful that we should again take the cup and drink?"

He said unto us: "Yea, it is needful, until the day when I come again, with them that have been put to death for my sake."

Then said we to him: "Lord, that which thou hast revealed unto us is great. Wilt thou come in the power of any creature or in an appearance of any kind?"

He answered and said unto us: "Verily I say unto you, I shall come like the sun when it is risen, and my brightness will be seven times the brightness thereof! The wings of the clouds shall bear me in brightness, and the sign of the cross shall go before me, and I shall come upon earth to judge the quick and the dead."

We said unto him: "Lord, after how many years shall this come to pass?"

He said unto us: "When the hundredth part and the twentieth part is fulfilled, between the Pentecost and the feast of un-leavened bread, then shall the coming of my Father be."

We said unto him: "Now sayest thou unto us: I will come; and how sayest thou: He that sent me is he that shall come?"

Then said he to us: "I am wholly in the Father and my Father is in me."

Then said we to him: "Wilt thou indeed forsake us until thy coming? Where can we find a master?"

But he answered and said unto us: "Know ye not, then, that like as until now I have been here, so also was I there, with him that sent me?"

And we said to him: "Lord, is it then possible that thou shouldest be both here and there?"

But he answered us: "I am wholly in the Father and the Father in me. . . . I am of his resemblance and form, of his power and completeness, and of his light. I am his complete Word. . . .

"And this preach ye also and teach them that believe on me, and preach the kingdom of heaven of my Father, and how my Father hath given me the power, that ye may bring near the children of my heavenly Father. Preach ye, and they shall obtain faith, that ye may be they for whom it is ordained that they shall bring his children unto heaven."

And we said unto him: "Lord, unto thee it is possible to accomplish that whereof thou tellest us; but how shall we be able to do it?"

He said to us: "Verily I say unto you, preach and proclaim as I command you, for I will be with you, for it is my good pleasure to be with you, that ye may be heirs with me in the kingdom of heaven, even the kingdom of him that sent me. Verily I say unto you, ye shall be my brethren and my friends, for my Father hath found pleasure in you: and so also shall they be that believe on me by your means. Verily I say unto you, such and so great joy hath my Father prepared for you that the angels and the powers desired and do desire to see it and look upon it; but it is not given unto them to behold the glory of my Father."

We said unto him: "Lord, what is this whereof thou speakest to us?"

He answered us: "Ye shall behold a light, more excellent than that which shineth. . . . And the Son shall become perfect through the Father who is Light, for the Father is perfect which bringeth to pass death and resurrection, and ye shall see a perfection more perfect than the perfect. And I am wholly at the right hand of the Father, even in him that maketh perfect."

And we said unto him: "Lord, in all things art thou become salvation and life unto us, for that thou makest known such a hope unto us." And he said to us: "Be of good courage and rest in me. Verily I say unto you, your rest shall be above, in the place where is neither eating nor drinking, nor care nor sorrow, nor passing away of them that are therein: for ye shall have no part in the things of earth, but ye shall be received in the everlastingness of my Father. Like as I am in him, so shall ye also be in me."

Again we said unto him: "In what form? in the fashion of angels, or in flesh?"

And he answered and said unto us: "Lo, I have put on your flesh, wherein I was born and crucified, and am risen again through my Father which is in heaven, that the prophecy of David the prophet might be fulfilled, in regard of that which was declared concerning me and my death and resurrection. . . .

"If, therefore, all the words which were spoken by the prophets have been fulfilled in me (for I myself was in them), how much more shall that which I say unto you come to pass indeed, that he which sent me may be glorified by you and by them that believe on me?"

And when he had said this unto us, we said to him: "In all things hast thou had mercy on us and saved us, and hast revealed all things unto us; but yet would we ask of thee somewhat if thou give us leave."

And he said unto us: "I know that ye pay heed, and that your heart is well-pleased when ye hear me: now concerning that which ye desire I will speak good words unto you. For

verily I say unto you: 'Like as my Father hath raised me from
the dead, so shall ye also rise and be taken up into the highest
heaven, unto the place whereof I have told you from the beginning, unto the place which he who sent me hath prepared
for you. And so will I accomplish all dispensations, even I who
am unbegotten and yet begotten of mankind, who am without
flesh and yet have borne flesh, for to that end am I come, that ye
might rise from the dead in your flesh, in the second birth,
even a vesture that shall not decay, together with all them that
hope and believe in him that sent me: for so is the will of my
Father, that I should give unto you, and unto them whom it
pleaseth me, the hope of the kingdom."

Then said we unto him: "Great is that which thou sufferest us
to hope, and tellest us."

And he answered and said: "Believe ye that everything that
I tell you shall come to pass?"

We answered and said: "Yea, Lord."

He said unto us: "Verily I say unto you, that I have obtained
the whole power of my Father, that I may bring back into light
them that dwell in darkness, them that are in corruption into
incorruption, them that are in death into life, and that I may
loose them that are in fetters. For that which is impossible with
men, is possible with the Father. I am the hope of them that
despair, the helper of them that have no saviour, the wealth of
the poor, the health of the sick, and the resurrection of the
dead."

When he had thus said, we said unto him: "Lord, is it true
that the flesh shall be judged together with the soul and the
spirit, and that the one part shall rest in heaven and the other
part be punished everlastingly yet living?"

And he said unto us: "How long will ye inquire and doubt?"

Again we said unto him: "Lord, there is necessity upon us to
inquire of thee—because thou hast commanded us to preach—
that we ourselves may learn assuredly of thee and be profitable
preachers, and that they which are instructed by us may believe in thee. Therefore must we needs inquire of thee."

He answered us and said: "Verily I say unto you, the resurrection of the flesh shall come to pass with the soul therein and the spirit."

And we said unto him: "Lord, is it then possible that that which is dissolved and brought to nought should become whole? We ask thee not as unbelieving, neither as if it were impossible unto thee; but verily we believe that that which thou sayest shall come to pass."

And he was wroth with us and said: "O ye of little faith, how long will ye ask questions? But what ye will, tell it me, and I myself will tell you without grudging: only keep ye my commandments and do that which I bid you, and turn not away your face from any man, that I turn not my face away from you, but without shrinking and fear and without respect of persons, minister ye in the way that is direct and narrow and strait. So shall my Father himself rejoice over you."

Again we said unto him: "Lord, already are we ashamed that we question thee oft-times and burden thee."

And he answered and said unto us: "I know that in faith and with your whole heart ye do question me; therefore do I rejoice over you, for verily I say unto you: I rejoice, and my Father that is in me, because ye question me; and your importunity is unto me rejoicing and unto you it giveth life."

And when he had so said unto us, we were glad that we had questioned him, and we said to him: "Lord, in all things thou makest us alive and hast mercy on us. Wilt thou now declare unto us that which we shall ask thee?"

Then said he unto us: "Is it the flesh that passeth away, or is it the spirit?"

We said unto him: "The flesh is it that passeth away."

Then said he unto us: "That which hath fallen shall rise again, and that which was lost shall be found, and that which was weak shall recover, that in these things that are so created the glory of my Father may be revealed. As he hath done unto me, so will I do unto all that believe in me.

"Verily I say unto you: the flesh shall arise, and the soul, alive, that their defence may come to pass on that day in regard of that that they have done, whether it be good or evil: that there may be a choosing-out of the faithful who have kept the commandments of my Father that sent me; and so shall the judgement be accomplished with strictness. For my Father said unto me: My Son, in the day of judgement thou shalt have no respect for the rich, neither pity for the poor, but according to the sins of every man shalt thou deliver him unto everlasting torment. But unto my beloved that have done the commandments of my Father that sent me will I give the rest of life in the kingdom of my Father which is in heaven, and they shall behold that which he hath given me. And he hath given me authority to do that which I will, and to give that which I have promised and determined to give and grant unto them.

"For to that end went I down unto the place of Lazarus, and preached unto the righteous and the prophets, that they might come out of the rest which is below and come up into that which is above; and I poured out upon them with my right hand the water of life and forgiveness and salvation from all evil, as I have done unto you and unto them that believe on me. But if any man believe on me and do not my commandments, although he have confessed my name, he hath no profit therefrom but runneth a vain race: for such will find themselves in perdition and destruction, because they have despised my commandments.

"But so much the more have I redeemed you, the children of light, from all evil and from the authority of the rulers, and every one that believeth on me by your means. For that which I have promised unto you will I give unto them also, that they may come out of the prison-house and the fetters of the rulers."

We answered and said: "Lord, thou hast given unto us the rest of life and hast given us joy by wonders, unto the confirmation of faith: wilt thou now preach the same unto us, seeing that thou hast preached it unto the righteous and the prophets?"

Then said he unto us: "Verily I say unto you, all that have believed on me and that believe in him that sent me will I take up into the heaven, unto the place which my Father hath prepared for the elect, and I will give you the kingdom, the chosen kingdom, in rest, and everlasting life.

"But all they that have offended against my commandments and have taught other doctrine, perverting the Scripture and adding thereto, striving after their own glory, and that teach with other words them that believe on me in uprightness, if they make them fall thereby, shall receive everlasting punishment."

We said unto him: "Lord, shall there then be teaching by others, diverse from that which thou hast spoken unto us?"

He said unto us: "It must needs be, that the evil and the good may be made manifest; and the judgement shall be manifest upon them that do these things, and according to their works shall they be judged and shall be delivered unto death."

Again we said unto him: "Lord, blessed are we in that we see thee and hear thee declaring such things, for our eyes have beheld these great wonders that thou hast done."

He answered and said unto us: "Yea, rather blessed are they that have not seen and yet have believed, for they shall be called children of the kingdom, and they shall be perfect among the perfect, and I will be unto them life in the kingdom of my Father."

Again we said unto him: "Lord, how shall men be able to believe that thou wilt depart and leave us; for thou sayest unto us: There shall come a day and an hour when I shall ascend unto my Father?"

But he said unto us: "Go ye and preach unto the twelve tribes, and preach also unto the heathen, and to all the land of Israel from the east to the west and from the south unto the north, and many shall believe on the Son of God."

But we said unto him: "Lord, who will believe us, or hearken unto us, or how shall we be able to teach the powers and signs and wonders which thou hast done?"

Then answered he and said to us: "Go ye and preach the mercifulness of my Father, and that which he hath done through

me will I myself do through you, for I am in you, and I will
give you my peace, and I will give you a power of my spirit,
that ye may prophesy to them unto life eternal. And unto the
others also will I give my power, that they may teach the
residue of the peoples.

"And behold a man shall meet you, whose name is Saul,
which being interpreted is Paul: he is a Jew, circumcised according to the law, and he shall receive my voice from heaven
with fear and terror and trembling. And his eyes shall be
blinded, and by your hands by the sign of the cross shall they
be protected. . . ."

And we said unto him again: "Lord, so many great things
hast thou told us and revealed unto us as never yet were spoken,
and in all hast thou given us rest and been gracious unto us.
After thy resurrection thou didst reveal unto us all things that
we might be saved indeed; but thou saidst unto us only: There
shall be wonders and strange appearances in heaven and on
earth before the end of the world come. Tell us now, how
shall we perceive it?"

And he answered us: "I will teach it you; and not that which
shall befall you only, but them also whom ye shall teach and
who shall believe, as well as them who shall hear that man
and believe on me. In those years and days shall it come to
pass."

And we said again unto him: "Lord, what shall come to pass?"

And he said unto us: "Then shall they that believe and they
that believe not hear a trumpet in the heaven, a vision of great
stars which shall be seen in the day, wonderful sights in heaven
reaching down to the earth; stars which fall upon the earth like
fire, and a great and mighty hail of fire. The sun and the moon
fighting one with the other, a continual rolling and noise of
thunders and lightnings, thunder and earthquake; cities falling
and men perishing in their overthrow, a continual dearth for
lack of rain, a terrible pestilence and great mortality, mighty
and untimely, so that they that die lack burial: and the bearing
forth of brethren and sisters and kinsfolk shall be upon one

bier. The kinsman shall show no favour to his kinsman, nor any man to his neighbour. And they that were overthrown shall rise up and behold them that overthrew them, that they lack burial, for the pestilence shall be full of hatred and pain and envy: and men shall take from one and give to another. And thereafter shall it wax yet worse than before.

"Then shall my Father be wroth at the wickedness of men, for many are their transgressions, and the abomination of their uncleanness weigheth heavy upon them in the corruption of their life."

And we asked him: "What of them that trust in thee?"

He answered and said unto us: "Ye are yet slow of heart; and how long? Verily I say unto you, as the prophet David spake of me and of my people, so shall it be for them also that believe on me. But they that are deceivers in the world and enemies of righteousness, upon them shall come the fulfilment of the prophecy of David, who said: Their feet are swift to shed blood, their tongue uttereth slander, adders' poison is under their lips. I behold thee companying with thieves, and partaking with adulterers, thou continuest speaking against thy brother and puttest stumbling-blocks before thine own mother's son. What thinkest thou, that I shall be like unto thee? Behold now how the prophet of God hath spoken of all, that all things may be fulfilled which he said aforetime."

And again we said unto him: "Lord, will not then the nations say: Where is their God?"

And he answered and said unto us: "Thereby shall the elect be known, that they, being plagued with such afflictions, come forth."

We said: "Will then their departure out of the world be by a pestilence which giveth them pain?"

He answered us: "Nay, but if they suffer such affliction, it will be a proving of them, whether they have faith and remember these my sayings, and fulfil my commandments. These shall arise, and short will be their expectation, that he may be glorified that sent me, and I with him. For he hath sent me unto

you to tell you these things; and that ye may impart them
unto Israel and the Gentiles and they may hear, and they also
be redeemed and believe on me and escape the woe of the
destruction. But whoso escapeth from the destruction of death,
him will they take and hold him fast in the prison-house in
torments like the torments of a thief."

And we said unto him: "Lord, will they that believe be
treated like the unbelievers, and wilt thou punish them that
have escaped from the pestilence?"

And he said unto us: "If they that believe in my name deal
like the sinners, then have they done as though they had not
believed."

And we said again to him: "Lord, have they on whom this lot
hath fallen no life?"

He said: "Whoso hath accomplished the praise of my Father,
he shall abide in the resting-place of my Father."

Then said we: "Lord, teach us what shall come to pass thereafter."

And he answered: "In those years and days shall war be
kindled upon war; the four ends of the earth shall be in
commotion and fight against one another. Thereafter shall be
quakings of clouds, darkness, and dearth, and persecutions of
them that believe on me and against the elect. Thereupon shall
come doubt and strife and transgressions against one another.
And there shall be many that believe on my name and yet
follow after evil and spread vain doctrine. And men shall follow
after them and their riches, and be subject unto their pride,
and lust for drink, and bribery, and there shall be respect of
persons among them.

"But they that desire to behold the face of God and respect
not the persons of the rich sinners, and are not ashamed before
the people that lead them astray, but rebuke them, they shall
be crowned by the Father. And they also shall be saved that
rebuke their neighbours, for they are sons of wisdom and of
faith. But if they become not children of wisdom, whoso hateth

his brother and persecuteth him and showeth him no favour, him will God despise and reject.

"But they that walk in truth and in the knowledge of the faith, and have love towards me—for they have endured insult —they shall be praised for that they walk in poverty and endure them that hate them and put them to shame. Men have stripped them naked, for they despised them because they continued in hunger and thirst, but after they have endured patiently, they shall have the blessedness of heaven, and they shall be with me for ever. But woe unto them that walk in pride and boasting, for their end is perdition."

And we said unto him: "Lord, is this thy purpose, that thou leavest us, to come upon them?"

He answered: "After what manner shall the judgement be? whether righteous or unrighteous?"

We said unto him: "Lord, in that day will they say unto thee: Thou hast not distinguished between righteousness and unrighteousness, between the light and the darkness, and evil and good?"

Then said he: "I will answer them and say: Unto Adam was power given to choose one of the two: he chose the light and laid his hand thereon, but the darkness he left behind him and cast away from him. Therefore have all men power to believe in the light which is life, and which is the Father that hath sent me. And every one that believeth and doeth the works of the light shall live in them; but if there be any that confesseth that he belongeth unto the light, and doeth the works of darkness, such an one hath no defence to utter, neither can he lift up his face to look upon the Son of God, which Son am I. For I will say unto him: As thou soughtest, so hast thou found, and as thou askedst, so hast thou received. Wherefore condemnest thou me, O man? Wherefore hast thou departed from me and denied me? And wherefore hast thou confessed me and yet denied me? hath not every man power to live and to die? Whoso then hath kept my commandments shall be a son of the light, that is, of the Father that is in me.

"But because of them that corrupt my words am I come down from heaven. I am the word: I became flesh, and I wearied myself and taught, saying: The heavy laden shall be saved, and they that are gone astray shall go astray for ever. They shall be chastised and tormented in their flesh and in their soul."

And we said unto him: "O Lord, verily we are sorrowful for their sake."

And he said unto us: "Ye do rightly, for the righteous are sorry for the sinners, and pray for them, making prayer unto my Father."

Again we said unto him: "Lord, is there none that maketh intercession unto thee?"

And he said: "Yea, and I will hearken unto the prayer of the righteous which they make for them."

When he had so said unto us, we said to him: "Lord, in all things hast thou taught us and had mercy on us and saved us, that we might preach unto them that are worthy to be saved, and that we might obtain a recompense with thee."

He answered and said unto us: "Go and preach, and ye shall be labourers, and fathers, and ministers."

We said: "Thou art he that shalt preach by us."

Then answered he us, saying: "Be not all fathers or all masters."

We said: "Lord, thou art he that saidst unto us: Call no man your father upon earth, for one is your Father, which is in heaven, and your master. Wherefore sayest thou now unto us: Ye shall be fathers of many children, and servants and masters?"

He answered and said unto us: "According as ye have said. For verily I say unto you: whosoever shall hear you and believe on me, shall receive of you the light of the seal through me, and baptism through me: ye shall be fathers and servants and masters."

But we said: "Lord, how may it be that every one of us should be these three?"

He said unto us: "Verily I say unto you: Ye shall be called fathers, because with praiseworthy heart and in love ye have revealed unto them the things of the kingdom of heaven. And ye shall be called servants, because they shall receive the baptism of life and the remission of their sins at my hand through you. And ye shall be called masters, because ye have given them the word without grudging, and have admonished them, and when ye admonished them, they were converted. Ye were not afraid of their riches, nor ashamed before their face, but ye kept the commandments of my Father and fulfilled them. And ye shall have a great reward with my Father which is in heaven, and they shall have forgiveness of sins and everlasting life, and be partakers in the kingdom of heaven."

And we said unto him: "Lord, even if every one of us had ten thousand tongues to speak withal, we could not thank thee, for that thou promisest such things unto us."

Then answered he us, saying: "Only do ye that which I say unto you, even as I myself also have done it. And ye shall be like the wise virgins which watched and slept not, but went forth unto the lord into the bridechamber: but the foolish virgins were not able to watch, but slumbered."

And we said unto him: "Lord, who are the wise and who are the foolish?"

He said unto us: "Five wise and five foolish; for these are they of whom the prophet hath spoken: Sons of God are they. Hear now their names."

But we wept and were troubled for them that slumbered.

He said unto us: "The five wise are Faith and Love and Grace and Peace and Hope. Now they of the faithful who possess these shall be guides unto them that have believed on me and on him that sent me. For I am the Lord and I am the bridegroom whom they have received, and they have entered in to the house of the bridegroom and are laid down with me in the bridal chamber rejoicing. . . ."

And we said unto him: "Lord, who then are the foolish?"

He said unto us: "Hear their names. They are Knowledge, Understanding, Obedience, Patience, and Compassion. These are they that slumbered in them that have believed and confessed me but have not fulfilled my commandments. On account of them that have slumbered, they shall remain outside the kingdom and the fold of the shepherd and his sheep. But whoso shall abide outside the sheepfold, him will the wolves devour, and he shall . . . die in much affliction: in him shall be no rest nor endurance, and although he be hardly punished, and rent in pieces and devoured in long and evil torment, yet shall he not be able to obtain death quickly. . . .

"But be ye upright and preach rightly and teach, and be not abashed by any man and fear not any man, and especially the rich, for they do not my commandments, but boast themselves in their riches."

And we said unto him: "Lord, tell us if it be the rich only."

He answered, saying unto us: "If any man who is not rich and possesseth a small livelihood giveth unto the poor and needy, men will call him a benefactor.

"But if any man fall under the load because of sin that he hath committed, then shall his neighbour correct him because of the good that he hath done unto his neighbour. And if his neighbour correct him and he return, he shall be saved, and he that corrected him shall receive a reward and live for ever. For a needy man, if he see him that hath done him good sin, and correct him not, shall be judged with severe judgement. Now if a blind man lead a blind, they both fall into a ditch: and whoso respecteth persons for their sake, shall be as the two blind, as the prophet hath said: Woe unto them that respect persons and justify the ungodly for reward, even they whose God is their belly. Behold that judgement shall be their portion. For verily I say unto you: On that day will I neither have respect unto the rich nor pity for the poor.

"If thou behold a sinner, admonish him betwixt him and thee: if he hear thee, thou hast gained thy brother, and if he hear thee not, then take to thee another, as many as three, and instruct thy brother: again, if he hear thee not, let him be unto thee as an heathen man or a publican.

"If thou hear aught against thy brother, give it no credence;

slander not, and delight not in hearing slander. For thus it is written: Suffer not thine ear to receive aught against thy brother: but if thou seest aught, correct him, rebuke him, and convert him."

And we said unto him: "Lord, thou hast in all things taught us and warned us. But, Lord, concerning the believers, even them to whom it belongeth to believe in the preaching of thy name: is it determined that among them also there shall be doubt and division, jealousy, confusion, hatred, and envy? For thou sayest: They shall find fault with one another and respect the person of them that sin, and hate them that rebuke them."

And he answered and said unto us: "How then shall the judgement come about, that the corn should be gathered into the garner and the chaff thereof cast into the fire?

"They that hate such things, and love me and rebuke them that fulfil not my commandments, shall be hated and persecuted and despised and mocked. Men will of purpose speak of them that which is not true, and will band themselves together against them that love me. But these will rebuke them, that they may be saved. But them that will rebuke and chasten and warn them, them will the others hate, and thrust them aside, and despise them, and hold themselves far from them that wish them good. But they that endure such things shall be like unto the martyrs with the Father, because they have striven for righteousness, and have not striven for corruption."

And we asked him: "Lord, shall such things be among us?"

And he answered us: "Fear not; it shall not be in many, but in a few."

We said unto him: "Yet tell us, in what manner it shall come to pass."

And he said unto us: "There shall come forth another doctrine, and a confusion, and because they shall strive after their own advancement, they shall bring forth an unprofitable doctrine. And therein shall be a deadly corruption, and they shall teach it, and shall turn away them that believe on me from my commandments and cut them off from eternal life. But woe unto them that falsify this my word and commandment, and draw away them that hearken to them from the life of the doctrine and separate themselves from the commandment of life: for together with them they shall come into everlasting judgement."

And when he had said this, and had finished his discourse with us, he said unto us again: "Behold, on the third day and at the third hour shall he come which hath sent me, that I may depart with him."

And as he so spake, there was thunder and lightning and an earthquake, and the heavens parted asunder, and there appeared a light cloud which bore him up. And there came voices of many angels, rejoicing and singing praises and saying: "Gather us, O Priest, unto the light of the majesty." And when they drew nigh unto the firmament, we heard his voice saying unto us: "Depart hence in peace."[1]

IDENTIFICATION OF SOURCES

Introduction

1. In *The Apocryphal New Testament,* by Montague Rhodes James (Oxford, England: The Clarendon Press, 1926).
2. Adolf Harnack. *Outlines of the History of Dogma* (Boston: Beacon Press, 1957).
3. Ibid.
4. G. R. S. Mead. *Fragments of a Faith Forgotten* (London: John M. Watkins, 1931).
5. Ibid.

Chapter I: The Mother of Jesus

1. Based on The Protevangelium in the version of *The Apocryphal New Testament* by William Hone which first appeared in 1820. Some paraphrasing has been used to clarify Hone's sometimes obscure translations.
2. Ibid.
3. Ibid.
4. Ibid.
5. From The Gospel of Bartholomew in James, op. cit.
6. From The Protevangelium in Hone, op. cit.
7. Ibid.

Chapter II: The Childhood of Jesus

1. Ibid.
2. Latin infancy gospel in the Arundel Manuscript. From *Latin Infancy Gospels,* edited by Montague Rhodes James. Cited by Edgar Hennecke in *New Testament Apocrypha* (Philadelphia: Westminster Press, 1963).
3. The Protevangelium in Hone, op. cit.
4. Latin text, The Gospel of Thomas in James, *The Apocryphal New Testament.*
5. James, op. cit.
6. Ibid.
7. Analysis of the Gospel of Pseudo-Matthew in James, op. cit.
8. From "The Discourse of Cyril of Alexandria" in James, op. cit.
9. The Gospel of Thomas in James, op. cit.
10. Ibid.

11. The Gospel of Pseudo-Matthew in James, op. cit.
12. Ibid.
13. From The Gospel of the Infancy of Jesus Christ in Hone, op. cit.
14. From The Life of John According to Serapion, translated by A. Mingana in *The Bulletin of the John Rylands Library*, Manchester, 1927. Cited by Hennecke, op. cit.
15. The Gospel of Thomas in James, op. cit.

Chapter III: The Lost Years

1. From *The Unknown Life of Jesus Christ from Buddhistic Sources*, by Nicolas Notovich, translated by J. H. Connally and I. Landsberg (New York: G. W. Dillingham, 1894).

Chapter IV: The Nature and Appearance of Jesus

1. From Epiphanius' *Work Against Heresies*. Cited by James, op. cit.
2. Origen on Matthew. Cited by James, op. cit.
3. Miscellaneous Coptic Texts. Cited in James, op. cit.
4. The Acts of John in James, op. cit.
5. Letter of Lentulus to the Roman Senate in James, op. cit.
6. Slavonic version of *On the Capture of Jerusalem*, by Josephus. Cited by Rupert Furneaux in *The Other Side of the Story* (London: Cassell, 1953).
7. From *The Sayings of Sri Ramakrishna*, compiled by Swami Abhedanada (New York: The Vedanta Society, 1903).
8. From The Koran, an explanatory translation by Mohammed Marmaduke Pickthall (New York: New American Library, 1960).
9. "The Oxyrhynchus Fragments." Cited in Mead, op. cit.
10. *The Secret Sayings of Jesus, the Gnostic Gospel of Thomas*, by Robert M. Grant, in collaboration with David Noel Freedman, with an English translation of The Gospel of Thomas by William R. Schoedel (New York: Dolphin Books, Doubleday & Company, Inc., 1960).
11. From The Acts of Paul in James, op. cit.
12. From *Irenaeus against Heresies*. Cited by James, op. cit.
13. Cited in James, op. cit.

Chapter V: Christ Crucified

1. From a fragmentary papyrus of the fourth, fifth, or sixth century. Cited by James, op. cit.
2. From The Acts of John in James, op. cit.
3. From The Acts of Pilate in James, op. cit.
4. From The Gospel of Peter in James, op. cit.

Chapter VI: The Resurrection

1. From The Acts of John in James, op. cit.
2. From The Story of Joseph of Arimathaea in James, op. cit.
3. From The Acts of Pilate in James, op. cit.
4. From the Ethiopic "Book of the Cock" in James, op. cit.
5. From The Gospel of Bartholomew in James, op. cit.
6. From The Acts of Pilate in James, op. cit.
7. From The Gospel of Peter in James, op. cit.
8. From The Acts of Pilate in James, op. cit.
9. From The Book of John the Evangelist in James, op. cit.

Chapter VII: The Later Appearances of Jesus

1. From The Acts of Peter in James, op. cit.
2. From The Acts of Andrew and Matthias in James, op. cit.
3. From The Acts of Thomas in James, op. cit.
4. From The Akhmim Fragment in James, op. cit.
5. Outline of a narrative attributed to Evodius. Cited in James, op. cit.
6. From The Acts of Thomas in James, op. cit.

Chapter VIII: The Books of the Gnostics

1. Mead, op. cit.
2. Cited in Mead, op. cit.
3. Cited in Hennecke, op. cit.

Chapter IX: The Fate of Pontius Pilate

1. From The Acts of Pilate in James, op. cit.
2. Appendixes to The Acts of Pilate in James, op. cit.
3. Appendixes to The Acts of Pilate in James, op. cit.
4. Ibid.

Chapter X: Last Words

1. From The Epistle of the Apostles in James, op. cit.